RUGBY
LESSON PLANS
FOR THREE-QUARTERS

with Jonathan Webb

Peter Johnson

A & C Black · London

First published 1994 by
A & C Black (Publishers) Ltd
35 Bedford Row, London WC1R 4JH

© 1994 Peter Johnson & Jonathan Webb

ISBN 0 7136 4041 3

A CIP catalogue record for this book
is available from the British Library.

Acknowledgements

Photographs on the front cover and on pages 4 and 62 courtesy of Professional Sport. Photographs on pages 12–13, 81 and 91 courtesy of Bristol United Press. Photographs on pages 35, 78, 79 and 102 courtesy of Sporting Pictures (UK) Ltd. Photographs on pages 65, 68–9 and 86–7 courtesy of Allsport UK Ltd.

Design and illustrations by Eric Drewery.

Typeset in 10½ on 12pt Trump Mediaeval by Intype, London.

Printed and bound in Great Britain by Hollen Street Press, Berwick upon Tweed.

CONTENTS

FOREWORD

I have been very fortunate to have experienced both the highs and lows of rugby union at virtually all levels of the game. The lows have been every bit as important as the highs.

In recent years the English national team has been transformed from also rans to double Grand Slam winners. Here is an excellent example of the benefits of good organisation and planning. With pretty much the same personnel, the quality of play was improved dramatically. This turnaround was not achieved overnight, but attention to detail and the use of exercises and drills such as those illustrated in this book have done wonders for the national side.

One of the most satisfying aspects of the sport for me was creating a game plan to beat a team, practising it, and then completing it successfully under pressure during a match. Pete Johnson's book will help with two of those steps. It will give you ideas about the patterns of play you might employ and it will show you how you can practise them without losing interest. Practising is hard work, but the drills in this manual will make it bearable because they are varied and progressive. The third step is down to the players on the pitch. With a clear picture of what you are trying to do, your actions will be significantly more purposeful, and inevitably more successful.

Above all, I hope this source book will permit you to enjoy your rugby more. The simple truth for me was the more I enjoyed myself the better I played!

INTRODUCTION

This book is a collection of lesson plans and structures, dealing with different aspects of rugby union three-quarter play.

It is designed for both coaches and players. The coach will gain immediate access to training sessions of 40 to 60 minutes for his three-quarters. Players will discover vital information about three-quarter play in defence, attack and counter-attack.

Each chapter kicks off with a relevant, in-depth explanation of the particular theme.

Each lesson is planned according to the principle of progression. It starts with simple, non-pressurised, individual exercises. The exercises become harder, involving more players and more pressure. The last exercise tends to be a unit drill involving the whole three-quarter line.

Each exercise is clearly explained. Key factors are highlighted – these are the coaching points that a coach will want to put over to the players. Also, there are hints on how long a coach can spend on each exercise in relation to the entire lesson.

We start with the organisation of defence. We then look at how to outflank and go through defences. There is a chapter on what happens once the first line of defence is breached. Another chapter deals with what happens when contact is made with the defence, and how important it is for three-quarters to support three-quarters and for them to link with the back row. Decision-making in broken play is the next section of this process. The last two chapters deal with going over the defence by kicking, and how to deal with these kicks and then launch counter-attacks.

Note Throughout the book rugby players and coaches are referred to individually as 'he'. This should, of course, be taken to mean 'he or she' where appropriate.

CHAPTER 1

The organisation of defence

MAN-FOR-MAN: LESSON 1

Whatever the defensive system employed by a three-quarter line, in the final analysis it all consists of man-for-man defence. Each three-quarter must be marking someone. The question is, who is marking whom?

In the defensive system generally known as man-for-man, it is usual for the first defender to mark the first attacker; the second defender marks the second attacker, and so on. Everyone counts the attackers from the inside to the outside, i.e. from the source of possession – such as a scrum – to the extremity – the wing. In the drift defence, it is the reverse. The outside defender stays on the outside attacker, and the defenders count the attackers from the outside to the inside.

Some teams like to use this man-for-man defence from all set piece play; others use it only from scrums. It is generally used in broken play situations, but much depends on the attackers' passing line. If the attackers pass too far away from the defenders, then the defenders can drift on to the outside attackers.

If an extra attacker is created, then the defending winger has to come in and leave the overlap player (usually his opposite number) to be picked up by a cross-cover defender, usually the full-back.

If the winger stays on the winger, he should be certain of a sweeper coming across to pick up the player he is allowing to run with the ball (say, the full-back coming into the line). However, since this is broken play, he cannot be certain of a sweeper; the cross-cover defenders may have been taken out by previous phases of play.

The midfield trio must move up together, taking the lead from the inside player. If one gets left behind or goes up more quickly than the rest, gaps will appear to be exploited by the attackers.

Approach the attacker from inside (on a path in the shape of a hockey stick – *see* diagram at the top of the next page) to

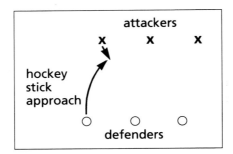

drive him across and outside. Accelerate quickly, run with control, and then accelerate into the tackle. Try to arrive at the same time as the ball, and tackle the ball, i.e. get a hand to it to prevent the pass.

If the attackers switch, defenders should stay in their zone or channel and not switch. A defender's channel is from his inside shoulder to the inside shoulder of the player outside him. Any ball carrier coming into this zone is his player. There is a time when the ball carrier becomes the next defender's responsibility, i.e. when the ball carrier crosses the 'T' with his own player (*see* diagram below).

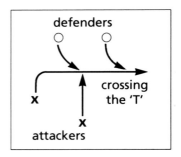

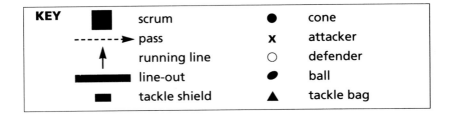

Lesson 1

Aim: to improve the man-for-man defence of the midfield.

Exercise 1

Work in fours. Holding hands, jog to the first marker and then jog backwards to the start line. Keep facing upfield, and keep abreast of each other.

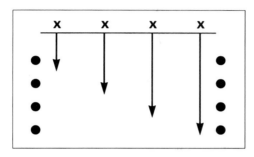

Progression: no longer holding hands, jog faster to each marker and back again.

Key points

- Keep level with each other going forwards and backwards. Look left and right.
- Work hard to get back into a defending position.
- Always face the ball and the opposition.

[5-7 minutes]

Exercise 2

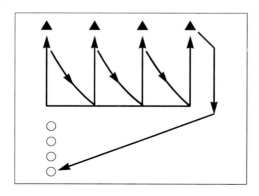

The first defender tackles the first bag, then drifts across, running backwards to the starting line. He then moves forwards again to tackle the next bag.

The second defender then joins in to tackle the first bag. Both go up together and back together. Then the third defender joins in, and then a fourth. When the first defender has finished, he re-joins the queue.

Key points

🌰 Take the lead from the inside player. Use a verbal cue.

🌰 Look inside and look to the front.

🌰 Keep level with each other.

[10 minutes]

Exercise 3

4 v 3. On the signal, four attackers run around a cone and attack the channel, while the defenders run around another cone and defend the channel. This can start off as one-handed touch rugby and progress to proper tackling.

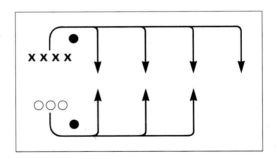

Much depends on the running angles and the passing abilities of the attacking group, but the emphasis is on the defenders to go man-for-man, and the attacking side *should* have the overlap to use.

Condition the defenders, and insist on man-for-man marking.

Progression: attackers can use switches and loops.

Key points

🌰 Go up together.

🌰 Take the lead from the inside player.

🌰 Count the attackers from the inside to the outside.

▰ The first defender tackles the first attacker, the second tackles the second, and the third takes the third.

▰ Always nominate the player by name, number or position. Make it clear which player you are going to tackle or two defenders may go for the same player.

▰ Zone defence.

[15-20 minutes]

ISOLATION: LESSON 2

Lesson 2

Aim: to create a second line of defence by using the blind-side winger as a sweeper.

Exercise 1

On the command 'Jog forwards', the shield-holders move forwards. The defending line (B) moves quickly to collide with and force the attackers in line A back to their original starting positions.

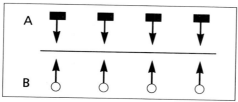

Key points

▰ Go up together.

▰ Timing. Hit the shields together.

[7-10 minutes]

Exercise 2

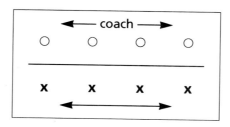

The coach stands behind the defenders so that they cannot see him. The attackers react to the coach's visual signals. When he moves left or right, they move in the same direction. When he holds up a ball, they move forwards.

The defenders stay on the attackers' inside, and react to the attackers' movements.

The 'inside' is: when the attackers are moving to the defenders' left, the defenders should tackle with their left shoulders; when the attackers are moving to their right, then they should tackle with their right shoulders.

A fail safe. The winger has worked hard to get back behind his full-back. From here he can be the full-back's eyes and the decision-maker. If the ball is dropped, the winger can sweep up the loose ball

Key points

- The 'hockey stick approach'. Approach from the inside of the attackers, pushing them out and forcing them to run across the pitch.

- Work together.

- Quickly use up the space between the two lines.

[10-15 minutes]

Exercise 3

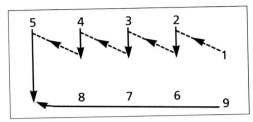

Player 1 (scrum-half) passes to 2. The ball is moved along the line to 5. Players 6,7 and 8 play man-for-man. 9 is the sweeper (blind-side winger) and he takes 5. Stage a race to see whether the ball can beat the sweeper, allowing 5 to score.

Progression: manufacture a break, e.g. let 8 cover 5 so 4 is free to break. 9 to take 4. Tell 8 to cover 5 and 7 to cover 4, so that 3 makes a break to be stopped by 9.

Key points

● The sweeper stays half-a-pass inside the ball.

● Other defenders turn and mark the support players so that the ball carrier has no-one to pass to.

[15 minutes]

DRIFT DEFENCE: LESSON 3

The drift defence is used often from line-outs, but it can also be used from scrums. It is not an excuse to avoid tackling!

Drift defence is easier to use from scrums on the left-hand side of the pitch. The open-side flanker will not have to worry so much about the back row and scrum-half. Most sides tend to attack to the defender's left-hand side of scrums, or pivot pass to the fly-half on the defender's right. So the flanker can basically concentrate on catching the fly-half who would be standing on the right.

With scrums on the right, the open-side flanker is concerned with the first player around the scrum, attacking to his left. This might be the scrum-half or someone from the back row. In this situation, the open-side has to check first that no-one is coming around before he can try and catch the fly-half.

There are several ways of operating. The midfield can start by covering their opposite numbers as if operating a man-for-man defence. As they go up, however, they can drift out on to the attacker outside so that the fly-half moves on to the inside centre. This means that the outside centre will cover the full-back coming into the line between the centre and winger.

The defenders could stand one out, i.e. the fly-half stands opposite the inside centre so that the defending outside centre stands in the space into which the attacking full-back will come.

Whatever the starting positions, the open-side flanker must deal with the attacking fly-half.

If the approach is slow to give the attacking side time to move the ball wide, the winger will be confronted by a wall of defenders. This also means that any move attempted by the attack will be made too early and the defenders will have time to adjust. The problem is that the attacking side will be given time to cross the gain line. A fast approach might be more advisable.

Lesson 3

Aim: **To improve the drift defence of the midfield.**

Exercise 1

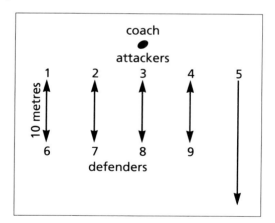

5 versus 4. No ball is needed by the players. On the signal, both lines jog towards each other. The defenders use holding tackles. The extra player always gets through. The attackers are to keep changing positions so that the defenders are tackling a different player each time.

Progression (i): coach to stand behind attacking line each time. He holds a ball. On the command 'Go', the attackers jog forwards. The coach holds the ball up in his right hand, the defenders stop players 1-4, and 5 jogs through. They are to imagine that 5 is the fly-half and the ball is going from their right to left as they are looking at it. When the coach holds the ball in his left hand, the defenders stop players 2-5 and 1 jogs through. They are to imagine 1 as the fly-half and the ball is travelling from left to right.

Progression (ii): scrum-half and ball at each end of the line. On the signal, the nominated scrum-half passes to the fly-half, and the three-quarter line attacks while the defenders operate the drift.

Key points

🏉 Count up the attackers from the outside in.

🏉 Last defender takes last attacker.

🏉 Approach from the inside to drive the attackers across the pitch.

[10-15 minutes]

Exercise 2

A back line is spread across the field and the players jog down their own channel as though they were playing sevens. As they move downfield they are to obey commands.

🏉 'Forward' – jog together and stay in a line.

🏉 'Right' – keep going forwards but drift to the right. The right winger stays on the same running line. All will then be running shoulder to shoulder, presenting a wall to the attackers wide out.

🏉 'Left' – as above but to the left.

🏉 'Back' – go back, re-aligning to original positions. Keep facing upfield. They are to imagine a second phase attack, and are rushing to get back into a defensive position.

This shows, in exaggerated form, the pattern of defence on the field. The ball comes out of the line-out and travels from left to right. The defenders drift to the right. There may be a maul or ruck and the defenders get back to their positions, waiting for the ball to emerge. When it does, it travels from right to left and the attack will be confronted by a number of defenders. Another passage of loose play takes place and the defenders run back to position.

Key points

⬤ Keep together going forwards and back.

⬤ Get back quickly to position.

⬤ Keep facing the ball and opposition.

[10 minutes]

Exercise 3

Play sevens in a confined area and at half pace. The defenders are always to have one player deep as a sweeper. The front line of defence is 6 confronted by 7 attackers.

The object is for the attackers to work the overlap by switching the direction of play and by looping. The defenders are to drift from side to side to prevent the overlaps. Use either touch rugby or holding tackles. Do not try to go forwards and make breaks, just work the overlap by playing laterally.

Progression: play 7 v 5 with two at the back, one to sweep and the other to play deep.

Key points

⬤ Count up the attackers from the outside in.

⬤ Outside player stays on outside player.

⬤ Nominate the player you are marking, and communicate with the other defenders.

⬤ Stay in a line.

[15-20 minutes]

CHAPTER 2

Outflanking the defence

ALIGNMENT AND SPACING: LESSON 4

The problems

There are major problems involved in outflanking a defence from a set piece. It is one of the hardest movements to achieve in rugby union.

The first problem is holding the midfield and open-side flanker close in to the set piece, preventing them drifting across on to the open-side winger.

Another problem is giving the winger enough space in which to operate, so spacing in the three-quarters and the width of the line are important.

Other factors that have to be considered are the speed at which the three-quarter line is moving over the ground, and how fast the ball is moving through the hands.

The relationships between the gain, tackle and passing lines are yet more problems. How deep the alignment starts does not matter quite so much as where the passing line is in relation to the tackle line.

Definitions

Alignment: the starting positions of the three-quarters whether in attack or defence. For the attacking three-quarters, they must consider their starting positions in relation to the tackle and passing lines.

Gain line: the point at which a team is moving forwards, i.e. an imaginary line through the middle of the scrum and line-out.

Passing line: where the attackers make their passes. This must be done before the tackle line is reached, or else passes cannot be made.

Tackle line: the collision point where the defenders meet the attackers. Assuming both lines are travelling at the same speed, this will be midway between the starting points of each line.

For example:

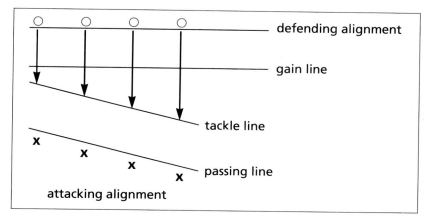

Apparent solutions

Most three-quarters will try to give themselves space in which to pass the ball by starting deep. This means that they will get their passes away without being caught with the ball.

If the ball then reaches the winger, other problems arise. What if he gets tackled? If he does, the ball is a long way across the other side of the field from where it started and also a long way back from the forwards. The team is losing ground.

If the three-quarters align deep, get the ball to the winger and he does not get tackled by his opposite number but is put clear, he is still going to find it difficult to outflank the second line of defence. The back row, blind-side winger or full-back will have plenty of time to get across the field because the winger has to cover a considerable distance before he gets to the gain line.

Perhaps the answer is the spacing in the three-quarters? If they stand wider, the ball can be given to the winger almost on the far touch line and it will be a long way for the cross cover to run, almost the width of the field. So everyone then starts spin passing because it is the best way to pass over a long distance quickly.

More problems arise. The spin pass cuts down the receiver's options. All he can do is concentrate on catching the bullet coming towards him. He will run away from the pass, drifting out to cushion the blow. It is also difficult to make long passes while running fast. The further away the passer and receiver, the more can go wrong with the pass itself. Since the passes occur a long way from the tackle line and the attackers are running slowly or even standing still to make their long passes, the defenders are not fixed; they can see what is happening and they can drift out to confront the winger with a wall of defenders.

Standing deep, throwing long, hard passes and trying to give themselves more space to make the pass, tends to force the three-quarters to run across field. This means that the ball carrier presents the easier side tackle to the defender; his support cannot see the ball because he is presenting his back to them; there is only one way he can run and so his options for beating a defender are reduced; he draws the defenders on to the players outside; the space in which the winger can operate becomes limited.

The solutions

The solutions, therefore, may be the opposite of all this. Rather than trying to relieve themselves of the pressure from the defenders, the three-quarters could actually accept the pressure. They could start shallow, not deep. This requires excellent handling skills.

To generate momentum and pace in the line, each player delays his run until the ball is in the inside player's hands. Then he will be accelerating on to the pass. The pass from fly-half to inside centre can be slightly deep, but the other passes are flat.

If anything goes wrong, the tackle line is close to the gain line and the support of the back row. The space is preserved on the outside. If the winger is put clear, the cross cover has less time to get to him and they will be running backwards, not forwards.

The three-quarters should stand close together so there is little that can go wrong with the pass. Even a bad pass can be caught. The further away the receiver gets, the less the margin for error with a bad pass. There is no need to spin pass. Reach for the ball, take it early and let the ball hang in the space for the receiver to run on to.

The running lines should be straight. Run at the defender to interest him and hold him where he is. This will prevent the defence drifting on to the outside players. The defender must cover his opposite number, who can step inside as well as outside him. He is also preparing himself for a possible head-on tackle.

The starting positions for each three-quarter should be with the hips square. The outside foot (i.e. the foot further from the ball) should be forward in the set position. When the player drives away it will be off the front foot and if the further foot is the front foot, he will immediately drive in towards the ball and thus straighten the line. He should also step in towards the pass, for the same reason. Getting the outside shoulder facing inwards will help to straighten the hips.

The fly-half runs straight and not across. He does not need to start far from the scrum-half because he wants to interest the back row. The scrum-half speeds up his pass but takes some of the weight off it. The fly-half too should not start his run until the ball is in the scrum-half's hands. He could also take the ball standing still.

The players must understand that the width of the pass must be the same, whatever the nature of the initial alignment.

Lesson 4

Aim: To make players aware of tackle and pass lines, spacing and alignment.

Exercise 1

In fives. The scrum-half is to pass and the ball has to go along the line to the end player before they cross the line in front of them. Call this the gain line although it is their own offside line if the scrum-half is passing from the base of a scrum.

The fly-half is only standing a few metres away from the scrum-half. The inside centre stands a little deeper, but outside centre and winger stand flat, almost level with the inside centre.

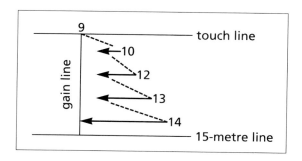

Place a cone opposite each player. The players must run at the cones. This will help them achieve a straight running line.

Progression (i): put down cones for a tackle line and tell the attackers to pass before the cones.

Progression (ii): have three tacklers coming slowly up on the attackers. Holding tackles only. Speed up the defence as the attackers become more proficient.

Key points

● Starting positions: outside foot forward; outside shoulder facing inwards; hips square.

● Reach for the ball and take it early.

● Step into the pass to keep on a straight running line.

● The pass should hang for the receiver.

● Delay the run until the ball is in the inside player's hands.

● Adjust starting positions in relation to your own pace and the pace of the inside payer.

[20 minutes]

Exercise 2

Start as for exercise 1. The ball gets to the end player and he puts the ball down on the gain line. Everyone is to run around the ball and come back along the same channel but in the opposite direction.

They must get the ball to the end player before crossing the gain line. All that the scrum-half has to do is run across after making his first pass, and make the second pass to the first player as he comes around.

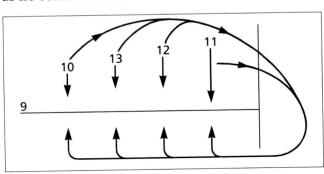

The three-quarters are now playing from second phase as though a ruck or maul had been formed and they are arcing around to its far side.

Progression (i): after the second pass, let the scrum-half act as opposition and the attackers must fix him.

Progression (ii): add opposition. 5 v 3. On the signal from the coach, the attackers and defenders sweep around to the other side of the ruck or maul. The scrum-half gives the ball and the defenders use a man-for-man defence (*see* relevant lesson).

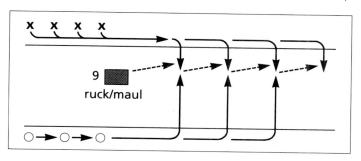

Key points

- Arc around and step into the pass.
- Get outside shoulders pointing inwards.
- Get on a straight running line before receiving the pass.
- First player around acts as fly-half. Fill up the space from inside to out, not outside in.
- Use soft, hanging passes.
- The ball carrier must slow as he makes the pass.
- Run at the defender.

[15 minutes]

Exercise 3

The three-quarters line up as if from a line-out on the half-way line. The ball is given out and the full-back enters the line. The ball eventually gets to the winger, who runs 10 metres and puts it down.

The three-quarters re-align on the far side of the ball, still moving in the same direction. The ball is passed to the end player, who runs 10 metres and puts the ball down.

The three-quarters re-align to switch back the other way, still going in the same direction. The ball is passed along the line with the full-back entering it. The winger runs 10 metres and the sequence ends.

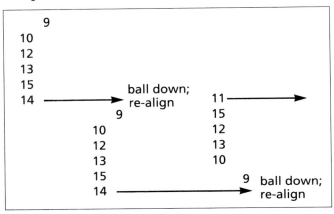

Progression (i): add a few defenders so that the attacking three-quarters can get their running and passing lines correct.

Progression (ii): the three-quarters can go through their moves, attack from second phase, going in the same direction, and then attack the open-side from third phase.

Key points

● Play to the edges and then switch back the other way.

● Key points for exercises 1 and 2 are relevant.

● Keep going in the same direction. Do not switch back too soon because you may bump into stragglers who will be put onside by the ball moving 5 metres.

● If outflanking has occurred from second phase, space should become apparent on the wide open side. Defenders will have been pulled across out of that area.

[15 minutes]

RUNNING LINES: LESSON 5

It is important for the midfield three-quarters to run at the inside shoulders of their opposite numbers. This line of running holds the defence close to the set pieces, saves the space on the outside for the full-back and winger to run into, and leaves the ball carrier with the option of beating his opposite number on his inside as well as on his outside.

If the attacking midfield players are running across, then they are presenting the easier side-on tackle to the defenders, and using up the space on the outside. They are drawing the defenders on to the runners on the outside, and they can only go for the outside break.

Hips must be square when the three-quarters are in their starting positions. If a player is standing side-on, with his feet wide apart and hands on knees, then there is only one direction in which he can start off running because his hips are locked.

Each player should be on a straight running line before he gets the ball. It is too late to straighten the line after giving the pass. This is usually done by sinking the hip and falling away from the pass. This should be in everyone's repertoire because the dummy pass is easy to execute. However, it does mean that it is difficult to support the pass because the player is going off in the opposite direction.

To get on this straight running line, it is better to step towards the ball. This means that each player has to continually re-position himself on the ball carrier. If he feels he is drifting away from him, he should step closer.

Straight running also means that the midfield has to be able to cope with the pressures involved. Their handling must be quick and accurate. This is made easier by standing close together. There is little that can go wrong with the handling, if the midfield is close. If they are wide, however, it means that the passes are wound-up spin passes. Much can go wrong with this – a spin pass coming at you like a bullet is a difficult pass to receive and pass on quickly. The longer the pass, the more of the body weight has to be behind it. That is the reason why so many players make fall-away, hip-sink passes. When this happens, the passer of the ball will find it difficult supporting the receiver. The passer is heading off in the opposite direction after the hip-sink pass. What matters is the speed of the ball through the hands, not the speed of the ball through the air.

The body moves through two planes as it is involved in passing. In the lower part of the body, the legs are pumping up and down along the vertical. In the upper body, the arms and shoulders are reaching for the ball to the side, and moving across the body along the horizontal. The hips are the axis for all this movement. They should not be moving; they should remain square-on.

Lesson 5

Aim: to improve running lines in order to fix defenders.

Exercise 1

In sevens. Players standing on the goal line, side-by-side so that each one can reach out with both hands and touch the finger-tips of the player on either side of him. Feet should be on the line, hips should be square and parallel to it. Just the shoulders should rotate.

The players are to walk together towards the 22-metre line and **hand on** the ball from one end to the other and back again. They do not pass the ball.

Progression: stand further apart, jog forwards and pass the ball.

Key points

- Reach for the ball.
- Rotate the shoulders.
- Keep your hips square.
- Re-position yourself on the ball carrier. If you are too far away, step closer to him.

[5 minutes]

Exercise 2

In fours, each group with a ball, players standing one behind the other in their corner, but outside a grid 10 metres square. Cones along the grid lines mark channels.

The ball is with a scrum-half in each corner. When he signals, all players step out and arc around as the ball is passed through everyone's hands to the end player.

Everyone has to be running fast. The ball has to get to the end within the width of the grid line; no-one is to cross the grid line. Thus the players stay within the touch line and preserve the space. The passes are made with some conception of the tackle line.

Now move to the next corner and move around the grid.

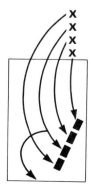

Key points

◗ Get wide very early. Work hard to do so before straightening the line, receiving the pass and feeding on.

◗ If necessary, the infield three-quarters must ease off the running speed to allow the wide players to get into position.

◗ Run on an arc.

◗ Step in towards the ball.

◗ Reach for the ball and take it early.

◗ Pass quickly and gently.

◗ Know where the touch and tackle lines are.

[10 minutes]

Exercise 3

In fours, each group with a ball and facing a channel. To the side of that channel and lined up one behind the other are tackle shield holders. The attackers run down the channel.

The first ball carrier steps in towards the first shield as the shield holder comes out to meet him. He makes his pass to the second ball carrier who steps in towards the pass and towards the second shield. When eventually the ball gets to the fourth player, one of the previous ball carriers has to be in a position to receive his pass.

Progression: get the shield holders' starting positions progressively wider so that eventually they will be standing opposite the four attackers.

Key points

- Keep the space on the outside.
- Get on to a straight running line by stepping towards the ball.
- Aim for the defender's inside shoulder to prevent him drifting out.
- Outside players must get wide quickly.

[15-20 minutes]

LOOPING TO CREATE THE OVERLAP: LESSON 6

Too many three-quarters regard their job to be over once they have passed on the ball. There is a tendency to stand back and see what the outside players can do with the ball, and either applaud or criticise their efforts. This is either due to laziness or because the passers of the ball find it too difficult supporting the ball carrier. Often the ball carrier makes life difficult for would-be support runners by running away from them.

If overlaps are to be created players must stand closer. This allows several things to happen. It is easier for the inside players to support the outside players because they do not have so far to run. The space is also kept on the outside for players to run into. A greater variety of options and deceptions can be employed, e.g. miss passes are available as an option, with the player missed out making the running off the ball.

If long passes are made, the space is used up, the passers cannot support the ball carrier quickly, and miss passes cannot be given.

To support the ball carrier quickly on the outside, the way the pass is given is also important. Hips should remain square, the fall-away pass **not** used. If the hips sink as the ball is passed, the passer is immediately falling away from the receiver and heading in the opposite direction. If the passer makes a follow-through pass whereby he immediately chases the ball, he may not fix the defender in front of him. He may draw the defenders on to the player outside. By keeping hips square and using shoulders and wrists in the pass only, it is possible to fix defenders and immediately follow in support.

A major principle of three-quarter play is that three-quarters should support three-quarters. It is unreasonable to expect the back row to support the ball carrier if he is wide out, a long way from the scrum, line-out, ruck or maul. Once a three-quarter has passed, his first thought must now be to follow the ball and work off the ball.

Lesson 6

Aim: to create extra players and overlaps by looping and developing into a ploy.

Exercise 1

Cyclic exercise in fives. Pass to one and loop two players, e.g. 1 passes to 2 and loops to receive pass from 3; he passes to 4 and loops to receive a pass from 5, etc.

Put down cones where the opposition might be, or put tackle shield holders there.

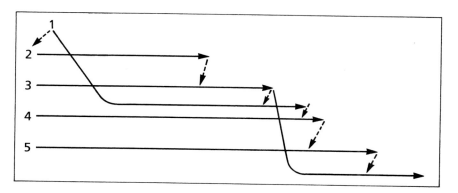

Progression: 1 passes to 2 and loops to the end of the line to receive a pass from 5. He passes back to 5 and loops to his starting place to receive a pass from 2. All change positions so everyone does the same exercise.

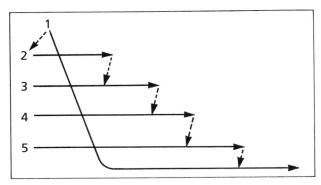

Key points

● Delay the run so there is space behind the ball carrier to get on a straight running line.

● Receiver runs on to the ball at pace to create space behind him.

● Ball carrier steps in to create space on his outside.

● Floating pass is given as looping player arrives on ball carrier's shoulder.

● Ball carrier slows and receiver injects pace.

● Outside player steps out to create space on his inside.

[12-15 minutes]

Exercise 2

Four attackers against five static defenders. If an overlap is to be created, then two players must attempt to loop.

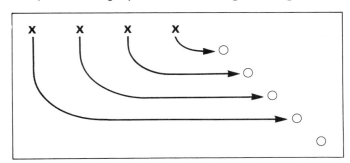

Progression: employ different starting positions. Stipulate that the attackers must beat the opposition by creating an overlap. The extra player runs up to the coach and gives him the ball. All the attackers have to run around the ball. The coach will give it to them as they run back the other way, and again try to create an overlap.

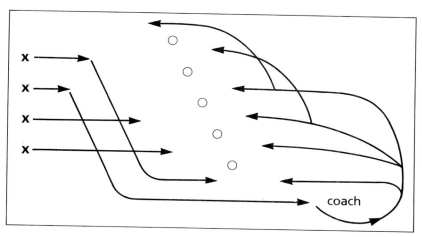

Key points

● Run on arcs. Step in towards the ball and aim at the inside shoulder of the defenders.

● Do not give the fall-away pass. Pass across the body but keep the hips square. It is easier to stop the ball carrier quickly.

● Give passes far enough away to fix the defender, but allow the next carrier of the ball time to get his pass away.

[20 minutes]

Exercise 3

Ploy: line-out or scrum. If a scrum, the spacing in the three-quarters will have to be very close.

The fly-half makes a miss pass, then passes to the outside centre. The fly-half and inside centre loop the outside centre. Decide who takes the inside and outside paths, but the outside centre has two players he can now pass to.

The midfield has been outflanked and if the defending winger comes in, then the overlap is created on the open side attacking wing.

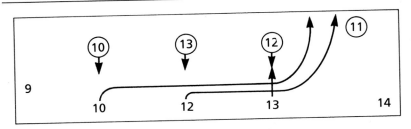

Key points

● The attacking midfield should stand close together so that the fly-half does not have a long way to go.

● Although initially accelerating, the outside centre may have to delay contact with the player marking him to allow time for the looping players to get into position.

● The ball carrier aims for the inside shoulder of his marker, but can move on to his outside shoulder as he makes the pass. This will prevent the defender moving out, so creating a hole for the receiver.

● The receiver enters the line with a change of pace.

● He should not arrive too early. He can come from depth and enter the line when the pass is being offered.

[10-15 minutes]

Exercise 4

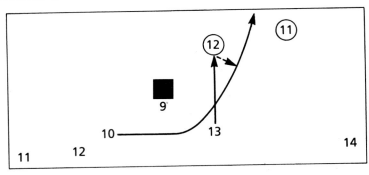

Ploy: scrum with a fairly wide narrow side. The scrum-half passes to the right centre who runs at his immediate opponent. The fly-half starts on the left side of the scrum and runs to get outside the right centre as he fixes his opposite number. If the defending left winger comes in to tackle the fly-half, then the overlap is created and the fly-half can pass to his right winger.

Key points

● The right centre takes a flat pass and runs inwards towards the inside shoulder of the tackler.

● The fly-half times his run to arrive before the ball carrier makes contact with the tackler.

● Soft, hanging pass into space for the fly-half to accelerate on to the ball.

● Support for the break comes from right winger and full-back.

[10 minutes]

CHAPTER 3

Penetrating the defence

CREATING THE EXTRA PLAYER: LESSON 7

There are two players who can come from deep and create two-on-one situations in the three-quarter line. These are the full-back and the blind-side winger.

There are five gaps into which these players can run: (1) is between scrum-half and fly-half; (2) is between fly-half and inside centre; (3) is between the two centres; (4) is between outside centre and winger; (5) is outside the winger.

Whichever gap these players intend running into, they should not stand opposite it. This is too much of a giveaway to the opposition. If they want to deceive them, they should start somewhere else and run on an arc to get into their intended gap as the ball is emerging from the set piece.

There should be communication between the three-quarters so that everyone knows where the extra player is coming into the line. Players should continue to stand close to each other as if nothing is happening. If they actually stand wide so that there is room for the extra player to come in, then this is a warning signal to the opposition.

The extra room is created by the player making the pass stepping in, and the player on the other side of the gap stepping out.

The player making the pass must slow down. If he is accelerating away, the player coming into the line will find it difficult to catch him up since he may be starting 10 metres behind the passer. The passer should take the ball up to the opposition quickly, then slow and offer the pass to the receiver who is running at full pace.

As part of the deception plan, the player giving the pass could dummy as if he were going to make a break himself, and then he could make the pass. He could make it seem that he is going to give a long wind-up pass, and then pop it up instead. Much depends on the space between him and the opposition line.

The extra player coming into the line. The ball is in two hands, ready for the pass when challenged. Note the defenders are swarming around to isolate the ball carrier and cut down those passing options

If the extra player coming into any of the spaces (1) to (3) above, then he will rarely have time to pass on the ball unless he makes a clean breakthrough. He must take the tackle and wait for the back row. His purpose was probably to disrupt the defence and create second phase possession. If he does achieve a breakthrough then he should be looking for immediate support because he will be confronted soon by the second line of defence.

If the extra player comes into spaces (4) and (5), then the purpose is usually to break through and create a 2 v 1 situation on the flank.

The pass to the player coming into the line in gaps (1) to (3) will be flat and soft. He will be running into these gaps almost on the ball carrier's shoulder. The ball carrier hardly needs to look to pass it to him; he should 'feel' him there. There will be more space in gaps (4) and (5), and so the distance between passer and penetrator will tend to be greater.

The full-back would tend to come into space (1) near his own goal line. His defensive and kicking abilities are useful here. The further from his own goal line, the wider he comes into the line, so that near the opposition's line he would be coming into gap (5).

If the full-back enters the line it is important to have a fail safe, so the blind-side winger would cover across behind the line. If you have confidence in the players and their handling ability or feel that in the event of an interception or dropped ball you will get players back in time to save a try, then overloading the attack and putting everyone into the line is not a bad idea.

Lesson 7

Aim: to show how and where to bring the full-back or blind-side winger into the three-quarter line.

Exercise 1

In fives, each group with a ball. Start one behind the other and arc out along a narrow channel. Pass immediately. Everyone must receive a pass within a distance of 7 metres. Come in close. The passer steps in to make room. Keep facing the front. There is no need to look, you know where he is. Get in front of the passer.

Progression: hand on one-handed to test concentration.

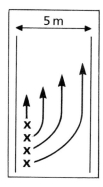

Key points

- Step in before making the pass to create space for the receiver.

- Make it a flat, soft, hanging pass.

- 'Feel' the player running on to the pass.

[7 minutes]

Exercise 2

In sixes, each group with a ball. Run down a channel 10 metres wide. Three are in front, three behind covering the gaps between the front three.

The three in front pass along the line to the end player. At that moment, the other line surges through, receives the ball, passes along the line to the end, and the first line comes through again. Continue like this for 40–50 metres.

Key points

- Accelerate on to the pass as you come through the front line.

- Slow down before offering the ball to the line coming through.

- There is a cycle of acceleration and slowing down.

[10 minutes]

Exercise 3

In sixes, with a ball, running down a channel 10 metres wide over a distance of 100 metres.

Four jog forwards, continually passing the ball back and forth. Two jog behind them. One of these works while the other briefly rests.

Player 1 decides where he is going to enter the line, enters at pace, calling for the ball. He slows, passes the ball back to the line again, and his partner decides when and where to come into the line while the first penetrator gets back into position behind the line.

All that the line has to do is jog and pass.

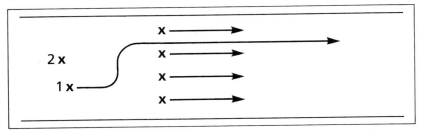

Key points

⬤ Come into the line at pace.

⬤ Communicate to those in front, where and when.

⬤ Do not run behind the gap you intend running into.

⬤ Your angle of run should be at an arc so that you straighten up as soon as you are in the line.

⬤ The pass should hang slightly. If the runner is coming in close on the shoulder, there is no need to look for him, just 'feel' him there.

[10 minutes]

Exercise 4

Employ a channel 5 metres wide. Groups of five. Acting scrum-half passes to the fly-half. Fly-half passes to the inside centre and loops the outside centre.

Progression: put down cones where the defenders would be. The attack will have targets to aim at.

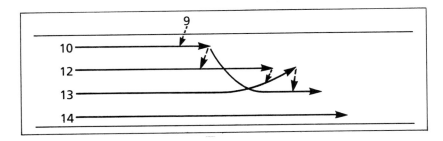

Key points

- Ball carrier steps in before giving the pass.
- Outside player steps out to make room for the looping player.
- Delay the run until you can get on to a straight running line.
- Accelerate on to the pass and get beyond the passer. This allows a player to get on to a straight running line. Otherwise there is no space behind the ball carrier, and the looping player has to run across and then forwards to get outside the ball carrier.

Exercise 5 [10-12 minutes]

The acting full-back or blind-side winger communicates to the players in front which space he intends coming into.

Do this exercise over a short distance, quickly returning to positions, with everyone rotating from time to time.

Progression: put down cones opposite the three players. Add opposition with tackle shields who are to come up slowly man-for-man on the fly-half, centre and winger.

Key points

- Passers put the ball into space.
- Passer steps in.
- Outside player steps out to make room.
- Extra player **not** to start opposite the gap he intends running into.

[10-15 minutes]

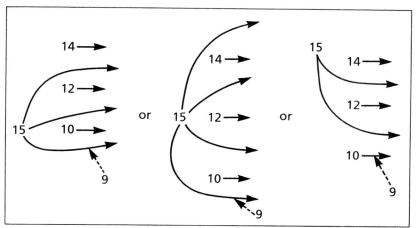

Exercise 6

Ploy: Miss out centre, inside pass and loop. Now the missed out player loops to appear on full-back's outside shoulder.

Progression: add defenders with tackle shields; one to cover the fly-half, one to cover the centre, one the winger, and one to act as cross cover to deal with the full-back.

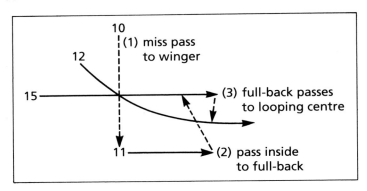

Key points

🏉 Winger slows before passing so that full-back can catch him up.

🏉 Full-back accelerates on to pass.

🏉 Centre delays his run so that he can get on to a straight running line.

🏉 Soft pass into space by full-back to the looping player.

🏉 Ball carrier to step in.

🏉 Full-back not to start in the same gap he intends running into.

[15 minutes]

LOOPING: LESSON 8

To create an extra player in the line, the passer of the ball can do a lot of running off the ball and come into the line again. In a sense, the passer can be the most effective player in achieving a breakthrough, because all eyes leave him after he has passed.

Wherever he intends entering the line again, he should delay his run until the players outside are past him and there is space behind them for him to get on to a straight running line. If a player follows the pass immediately and heads off towards the touch line, by the time he turns to get on a forward running line, a big space has developed between him and the players outside. He will find it difficult to catch up.

To generate space behind them for the looping player to get on the correct running line, the receivers of the ball must be accelerating on to the pass.

To give space on the outside to the looping player to come into the line, the ball carrier must step in. The player outside him should step out to give more space on his inside.

The ball carrier should aim at the inside shoulder of his immediate opponent to stop him drifting on to the looping player. He could step out to the outside shoulder of the tackler at the moment of making his pass, thus keeping him away from the player coming in. The ball carrier could then put the player into the hole behind the tackler.

The player coming in will be on the shoulder of the ball carrier, so the pass will be flat, soft and hanging in the space for the receiver to run on to.

The ball carrier must slow just before giving the pass so that the receiver can catch up, and also so he creates a change of pace in the line by bursting on to the ball.

The passer will be facing the front so that he can scan the field in front and fix defenders. This may be difficult from scrums where the two three-quarter lines are closer and the passer will be under considerable pressure. He may decide, therefore, to turn his back to the opposition and give a shielded pass. He should turn towards the looping player so he can see the ball all the time as he is coming around.

Lesson 8

Aim: to review the basic principles of looping to create extra men, and to utilise the loop in a ploy from a scrum and a ploy from a line-out to penetrate a defence.

Exercise 1

In eights, each group with a ball. Four players stand one behind the other and facing the other four similarly lined up 10 metres away.

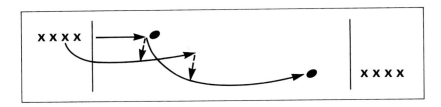

The ball is on the ground 2 metres out. The players operate in pairs. The first player runs out, lifts the ball and gives a pop-up pass to his partner who is running on to the pass at pace. He must then loop around his partner to receive a return pass and then place the ball 2 metres out in front of the other line of players. A pair from that group does the same and the cycle continues.

Key points

⬤ Bend the knees. Step beyond the ball. Lead with one shoulder behind the ball when lifting it.

⬤ Pop the ball into space so that it is hanging there momentarily for the support runner to run on to it.

⬤ Delay the run until the ball carrier is in front to get a straight running line.

⬤ Ball carrier steps in to make space to the side for the looping player.

⬤ Ball carrier to slow slightly so there is a change of pace as the looping player bursts on to the ball.

⬤ Another soft, hanging pass.

[7-10 minutes]

Exercise 2

In waves of five. A cyclic exercise running over a long distance.

1 passes to 2 and loops behind him to receive a return pass. 1 then passes to 3 and does the same with each of the others in the group.

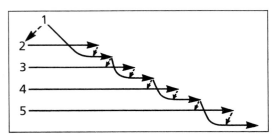

Progression (i): all loop. Pass to the next player and loop to the end of the line.

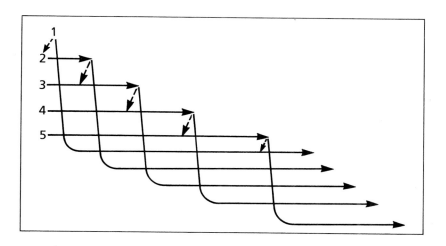

Progression (ii): miss one and the player missed out is to loop. 1 passes to 3; 2 loops to receive a pass from 3; 2 passes to 5; 4, who has been missed out, loops to receive a pass from 5. He passes back inside a miss pass and the cycle begins again.

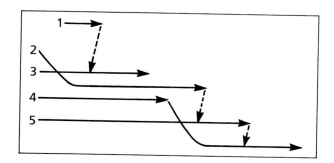

Progression (iii): miss one and double loop. 1 passes to 3; 1 and 2 loop 3; 1 takes the inside route and 2 takes the outside lane; 1 receives a pass from 3 and passes on to 2; 2 passes to 5, and 2 and 4 loop 5; 2 takes the inside and 4 takes the outside path; 2 receives the return pass from 5.

Progression (iv): 1 can take the outside path and 2 can take the inside track. Ball carrier can pass to either player.

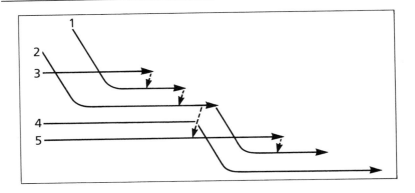

Key points

● Looping player delays run until ball carrier is in front. He can then get on to a straight running line.

● Ball carrier steps in, and outside player steps out, to create the space for looping player to come into the line. Looping player comes into the line at the shoulder of the ball carrier and arcs around.

● Soft, hanging pass so receiver can run on to the ball.

● Ball carrier slows as receiver bursts on to the ball.

[15-20 minutes]

Exercise 3

Ploy: line-out. Fly-half passes to inside centre and loops. He receives the pass and then passes to the blind-side winger who then passes to the full-back. The full-back can draw the defence wider by calling for the ball and distracting attention.

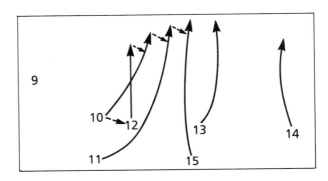

Practise the move without opposition and then involve two three-quarter units against each other. For the sake of continuity, if either move breaks down play second phase. The ball is to be recycled to the attacking side on the count of five.

Key points

🏉 Fly-half delays his run to arrive at pace on the shoulder of the ball carrier (12) just before he makes contact with the opposing inside centre.

🏉 Ball carrier runs at the inside shoulder of his opposite number to fix him, and then gives a hanging pass.

🏉 Blind-side winger runs on an arc. Arrive late rather than early. Come from depth and read what is happening in front.

🏉 Ball carrier slows just before giving pass. Receiver injects pace on to the ball.

[10 minutes]

Exercise 4

Ploy: line-out, scrum or static second phase. Fly-half misses out the inside centre and passes to the outside centre. The inside centre loops. The outside centre dummies a pass to the looping player and gives a pop pass to the full-back coming straight up the middle, outside him but inside the looping player. The full-back will have the inside centre in support.

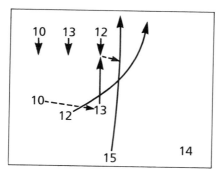

Key points

🏉 Fly-half passes early.

🏉 Outside centre runs at opposing centre to hold him there.

🏉 Inside centre has to loop wide.

⬤ Full-back times his run as he sees contact approaching and the outside centre offering the pass.

⬤ Full-back has inside centre and winger in support on the outside, and fly-half on the inside.

[10 minutes]

SWITCHING DIRECTION: LESSON 9

There are several ways of changing the direction of running to create a hole in the defence through which to put a ball carrier.

In all of these, the ball carrier is the player responsible for creating the hole by changing his angle of run. He must start by running straight and then look as though he is attempting to run outside/inside his defender by changing direction and running on a diagonal. This will draw his defender with him.

Once the ball carrier is taking the running space of another player, that player should switch channels with the ball carrier and aim for the hole left by the defender.

The player switching is the decision maker. He can see what is happening in front, while the ball carrier's field of vision is impaired by running across.

If the ball carrier dummies a pass to the player changing channels, it is often because he senses what is happening – that his opponent has stopped following and is waiting for the player on the switch. It may be part of a planned move but the dummy rarely occurs because the ball carrier can see what is happening.

The pass by the ball carrier will be soft and shielded from the defender. His back will prevent the defender from seeing the ball, and so the dummy is a valid option. The switching player will also see the ball all the time. If the tackle takes place, the ball will not get smothered and can still be passed.

The angle of run of the receiver decides whether this will be a 'switch' or 'scissors'. If he runs also on a diagonal, it will be a scissors. The aim is to look for support from the forwards. If the angle of run is straight, parallel to touch, then this is a switch. Its aim is to penetrate the defence and then look outside for support from the three-quarters.

There is also another switch – the outward switch. The outside player receives the ball and changes direction by running back in towards the passer. The inside player who made the initial pass then switches outwards with the ball carrier. Not quite the loop, but similar. It is the angle of run of the ball carrier that differentiates between this switch and the loop.

Lesson 9

Aim: to demonstrate the differences between the inward switch and the scissors.

Exercise 1: the scissors

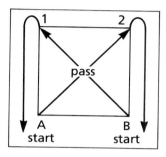

A line of players at A and B of a grid 10 x 10 metres. The players at A are holding a ball each. One player from A and B go at the same time. Player B runs behind player A to take a shielded pass. They continue to their opposite corners and then come back outside the grid to join the other queue.

Progression: players in each corner as in the Auckland drills. Ball at B. Players from A and B run at the same time and scissors in the middle. The ball is taken on to corner 2 and handed on. A player from corner 2 runs out and scissors with a player from corner 1 so the ball ends up again at B, etc.

Key points

- Ball carrier runs straight and then changes his angle of run.

- He makes a diagonal run.

- When he offers the pass, it should be shielded from the opposition so that the receiver sees it all the time; the ball will be protected by the ball carrier's body if the potential tackler makes the hit.

- The receiver to run on a diagonal and look inside for his support.

- Communication should take place.

[10 minutes]

Exercise 2: the switch

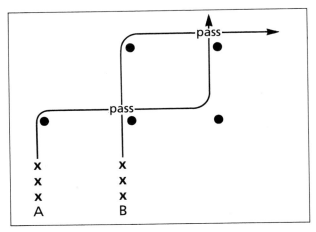

Player from A and player from B go together. A has the ball. He runs around the first cone and heads for the second cone, running across the line of run of the player from B. A pass is made as they meet. B goes on to the next cone, runs around that and changes his angle of run and crosses the line of run of A. Another switch pass is made and they both re-join the queues.

Progression: in fives with a ball. A cyclic exercise. Working a way down a channel, the length of the pitch or over 50 metres depending on the intensity of the exercise.

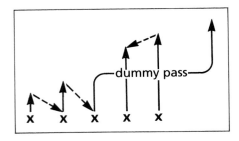

The ball is moved along the line from the left until it gets to the middle player. He runs across and does a dummy switch with the next player and an orthodox switch with the end player. The end player then passes back outside to the original ball carrier. He now passes back inside and the process starts again but with a new middle player. He runs across the field from right to left, dummy switches with the next player and switches with the outside player.

The middle player always makes a dummy and then an orthodox switch.

Key points

◆ Ball carrier to run straight and then change his angle of run across the pitch, either at right angles or on a diagonal.

◆ Shield the ball from the tackler.

◆ When he takes the running space of the outside player, the outside player should switch back inside on a straight running line.

◆ The receiver should then look back outside for support.

◆ The receiver decides when to start his run and demand the ball. He can scan the field in front more easily than the ball carrier.

[10 minutes]

Exercise 3

In fives. A move.

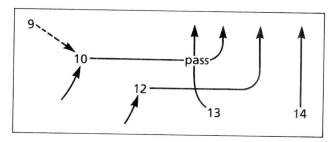

Fly-half starts running straight then changes to running across on a diagonal. The inside centre does the same so that they are running side by side. The outside centre comes back on a straight running line to receive a pass from the fly-half. He then links up with the outside players. This should be the outside centre and winger; the fly-half might have been tackled – if not, he could also get out there.

Key points

◆ Make this move from line-outs when there is time and space.

◆ Fly-half starts on a straight running line and then changes to a diagonal line.

● The inside centre must go with him to give the outside centre room to run behind.

● A shielded pass is given.

● The new ball carrier should look outside for immediate support.

[15 minutes]

Exercise 4

In eights. Five three-quarters with three back-row forwards. The three-quarters attempt to score against each other by switches, scissors or the move. If a breakdown occurs, play second phase. Coach counts from one to five and the ball is released for a second strike.

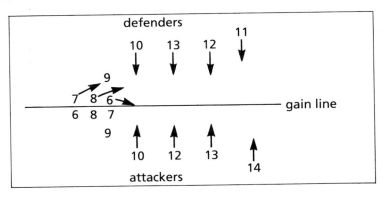

Key points

● If a scissors, look for the back row.

● If a switch, look outside for the three-quarters to support.

● If the move, look outside for support if on a straight line.

[15-20 minutes]

OUTWARD SWITCH AND RUN-AROUND: LESSON 10

The differences between the outward switch and the loop lie in the angle of run of the two participants and where the pass takes place.

With the loop, the ball carrier is running straight. He steps in to create room on the outside as the receiver turns up on the outside. The looping player will also be running on a straight line. The pass is given flat and to the outside of the ball carrier, who continues to face the front.

For example:

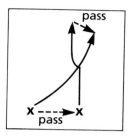

With the outward switch, the ball carrier runs back inwards on a diagonal line. He passes to the receiver, who is running also on a diagonal line but going outwards. The pass is shielded and given behind the ball carrier.

For example:

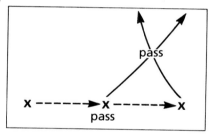

The run-around is similar again to the outward switch and loop. However, the difference is that the pass from the outside player is back inside. The receiver then runs around the original passer. This is technically legal so long as the player who is being run around does not deliberately attempt to protect the ball carrier and step in the way of a potential tackler.

For example:

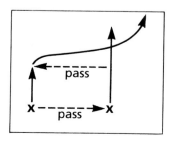

Lesson 10

Aim: to demonstrate the differences between the outward switch and the run-around and to introduce both into ploys for the three-quarters.

Exercise 1

```
B   X     X     X     X

A   X     X     X     X
          ↑
          ↓
1   X     X     X     X

2   X     X     X     X
```

In fours. A ball with the end player in group A. When group A has finished with the ball it is handed on to group 1, then handed on to group B and then group 2 in a simple relay.

Outward switch

As group A runs forwards, the ball is passed to the end player who runs back in on a diagonal and makes an outward switch with the player inside him. The ball carrier now hands the ball on to the next group and the cycle continues with each group.

Progression: the first player in the line passes to the second; the second player misses out the third and passes straight to the fourth; the ball carrier makes an outward switch with the player who was missed out.

Run-around

Progression (i): when the ball gets to the fourth player, he passes back inside to the third player who then runs around him.

Progression (ii): 2 misses 3 and passes to 4; 4 passes back inside to 3 who runs around 4.

Key points for the outward switch

- Ball carrier runs back on a diagonal line.
- Ball carrier shields the pass.
- Receiver runs a diagonal to receive the pass just behind the ball carrier.

Key points for the run-around

● Take care not to give a forward pass.

● Passer should stay and watch the ball carrier run around him and do nothing to give away a penalty.

● Ball carrier to run on an arc, using the passer as a shield and straightening up as he runs around him.

[15 minutes]

Exercise 2

In fives with a ball. Keep changing positions. One to act as a scrum-half, one as a fly-half, one as inside centre, one as outside centre and one as a full-back.

Players should practise the run-around to beat a drift defence.

The fly-half passes to the inside centre, who then runs on a diagonal back towards the fly-half and passes to him. The fly-half now runs around the inside centre. To straighten the attack, the fly-half then passes to the full-back who is on a straight running line.

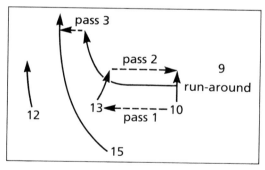

Key points

● Fly-half delays his run.

● Inside centre runs back to fix the opposition fly-half and back row.

● Inside centre passes back inside and fly-half runs around him.

● Full-back does not stand in the space that he intends running into.

● Full-back straightens the line.

[10 minutes]

Exercise 3

In fives with a ball. Keep changing positions. Scrum-half, fly-half, inside centre, outside centre and full-back required.

Outward switch to fix a drift defence.

Fly-half passes to outside centre. Outside centre runs back on the diagonal. He does an outward switch with the inside centre, who was missed out. The full-back comes into the line to straighten the attack.

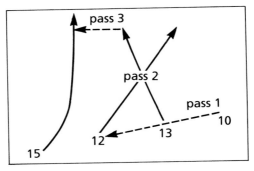

Key points

◗ Full-back stands outside the winger to run back in and straight.

◗ The outside centre gives a shielded pass to the inside centre.

[10 minutes]

Exercise 4

Two three-quarter lines in opposition. Five lives each to score, using either of the two moves.

[15 minutes]

CHAPTER 4

After the breakthrough

REACTION TO THE BREAK: LESSON 11

Once the defending line is breached, the ball carrier should be looking around for someone to make a pass to. It will not be long before he is confronted by cross-cover defenders.

There should be immediate support available to the ball carrier. The attacking players should aim at a spot 10 metres in front of them and try to get to it as quickly as possible. They will be surging through in numbers and ready to help.

If the line is broken by a planned move, the ball carrier should know who will be in support. That will have been planned too.

Lesson 11

Aim: to improve the support of the ball carrier who has broken through the defending line.

Exercise 1

In twos with a ball. Three tackle shield holders required.

The ball carrier aims for the gap between the first pair of shields and breaks through. He is then confronted by the single tackle shield and he makes a pass to his partner before the contact takes place. His partner scores.

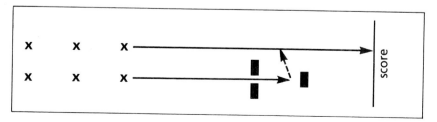

Progression (i): the ball carrier chooses which side to pass to and the support runner must react.

Progression (ii): the tackle shield at the back can now come from the side, so the ball carrier has to step towards him to hold him there.

Progression (iii): go in threes, with one player on either side of the ball carrier. The ball carrier makes contact with the single defender and puts the ball down. The inside support player comes in, lifts the ball and passes to the outside player who is running on to the pass.

The outside player could come back inside on a switch with the acting scrum-half.

Key points

● Lead with one shoulder through the gap.

● Protect the ball.

● Immediate support but hang back until the pass is offered so that you are running on to the ball.

● Make a flat pass.

● Ball carrier to run at the defender to hold/fix him and preserve the space outside.

[10–15 minutes]

Exercise 2

Two grids, each 10 x 10 metres. Two defenders in each grid and four attackers. The attacking players have to get through both grids, turn around immediately and score on the line they started from. They go again and do this without stopping for a minute. How many scores can they get?

The ball carrier will find himself isolated on occasions as the support players get left behind by tackles.

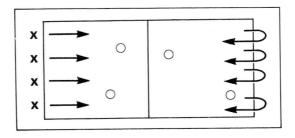

Key points

● Support the ball carrier.

Receive the pass running fast. Come from deep or delay the run until the pass is offered.

Ball carrier to delay contact if support is not available.

Ball carrier to go looking for support runners. Do not surrender the ball by being tackled. If there is no one to pass to, stop and come back.

[20 minutes]

Exercise 3

Two three-quarter lines in opposition. One line defends. The coach nominates a player of the defending side to drop back out of the line as the rest of his line go up to tackle. A hole will be left and the attacking side has to read it and put a ball carrier through the gap. The player who was told to drop back now defends with his full-back and blind-side winger. The other defending players try to bump their opposite numbers to prevent them getting through to help the ball carrier. They play no more part in the exercise after that.

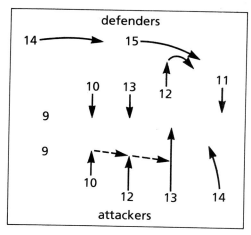

Key points

Immediate support of ball carrier. Get there!

Ball carrier to look for support.

Ball carrier to avoid contact until help arrives.

[20 minutes]

DEALING WITH THE CROSS COVER: LESSON 12

There are three types of defender: those who go up, those who go across and those who go back. If a team is attacking through the three-quarters, the first line of defence is the midfield who go up to tackle their opposite numbers. There is then another line of defence which is sweeping across behind the midfield. This would be the back row and blind-side winger.

How does one deal with this second line, the cross cover, once the first line has been broken?

There must be immediate support of the ball carrier, so the whole three-quarter line has to accelerate through. The ball carrier should not run away from them. His first priority after the breach is to look around for someone to pass to. Sometimes this may mean wandering about looking for support and not running straight. Slowing down is another option.

If the ball is moved immediately to the wing, it may work because the winger may be very quick and elusive and may want the extra time and space. However, care must be taken. Passing too early or giving miss passes may lose a possible 3 on 2 or 2 on 1 situation. It means that cross-cover defenders have only to set their sights on the one player and head for him. If the ball carriers pass only when confronted, the cross cover have continually to re-align themselves on new targets.

Generally, the ball carrier should not run away from the cross cover. If he does then he crowds out the outside players and intrudes into their space. He draws the defenders on to the outside players and, if caught with the ball, he presents his back to any supporting back-row players.

Run at the cross cover and give the pass at the best possible time. The space on the outside is preserved, and the defender is held or fixed or drawn. Do not slow down. Run at pace at him.

If the ball carrier finds he is running across, a support player on the outside can hold the defence by switching back inside on a dummy run.

Lesson 12

Aim: having broken through the first line of defence, to fix the cross cover.

Exercise 1

In fours with a ball and jogging down a line one behind the other towards a marker. When you get to the marker, arc around to attack at speed the stationary defenders on the other side of the channel. Everyone to receive a pass within the width of that channel.

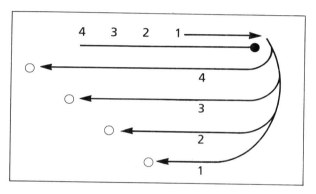

Key points

⬤ Run at defenders, not away from them.

⬤ Step in towards the ball, thereby establishing a straight running line before receiving the pass.

⬤ Keep your hips square.

⬤ Reach for the ball and keep close.

⬤ Preserve the space on the outside.

[7-10 minutes]

Exercise 2

Two sets of three-quarter lines in groups of four. A scrum-half in the middle with two balls. Three defenders, one behind the other, in front of the scrum-half. Another defender is starting deep in front of group A and one in front of group B.

The scrum-half gives the ball to group A. The first defender is to go for the first attacker; the second defender for the second attacker; the third defender for the third attacker. If the attacking three-quarters have been successful, they will get the ball to the overlap who has now to beat the single defender who started deep.

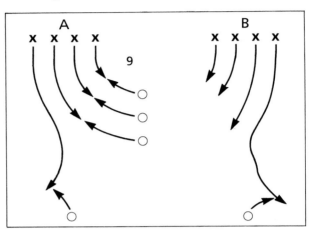

On the signal from the coach, 'Break', the three defenders have to leave group A alone and run back across the channel to defend against group B. At an opportune time, the coach will tell the scrum-half when to give the other ball to group B. Group B must now score against the cross cover and deep defender.

The defenders can go for any ball carrier to prevent the score.

Key points

● Run at the inside shoulder of the defender.

● Keep the space on the outside and get players running into it.

● Do not pass too early or too late.

● If the pressure is on you, make the pass.

● If the pressure is on the player on the outside, do not make the pass.

● Defenders stay inside the ball; do not overrun it.

● Defenders communicate in defence and nominate the players they intend marking.

[20 minutes]

Exercise 3

One three-quarter line with a ball.

The ball is passed along the line to the end player who runs up to the coach and hands him the ball. The coach puts the ball down and the line re-aligns to switch back the other way. The full-back can now come into the movement. The winger runs around the coach and tries to stop the line from scoring.

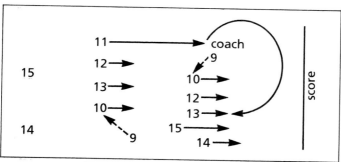

Progression: nominate another player to run around the coach to defend. Then nominate two players, etc.

Key points

● Run at the defender. Do not allow him to drift across.

● Keep the space on the outside.

● If you have a flying winger and want him to have room for a clear run in to the line, get the ball to him early. However, remember that a 3 v 2 situation can also become a 1 v 1 situation if a miss pass is used (i.e. from 1 to 3). The timing and spacing between the players is important here.

● If the pressure is on you, pass. If the pressure is on the outside player, do not pass.

● In the re-alignment phase there might be some disorganisation depending on which players have been told to run around and defend. Everyone has to slot in wherever they can. Communication must take place and if the blind-side winger is trying to get involved, he should not have to run to the far end of the line. He can quite easily shout out that he intends coming into the line and the players around the nominated gap can make room for him.

[20 minutes]

Surrounded by defenders, striving to stay on his feet and keep possession of the ball. Where are his fellow three-quarters? Three-quarters support three-quarters: if one is caught with the ball, the nearest three-quarter must go in to help

CHAPTER 5

Contact with the opposition

BALL RETENTION: LESSON 13

Rugby union is not a 'contact' sport for the three-quarters. It becomes a collision sport here because the two lines are running full tilt at each other. When the tackles are made, the ball carrier must control the ball and not lose it.

It is the responsibility of the player who made the pass to see the ball through the receiver's hands. The passer must go in and help retain the ball or move it on immediately. It is unrealistic to expect the back row to support a three-quarter who has been caught wide out. Three-quarters must support three-quarters.

Three-quarters must stay on their feet in the tackle and look inside for support. This means straight running so that the ball is always in the sight of the inside players.

Three-quarters should be involved in all the normal contact drills of forwards which take place after the warm-up. They must learn how to fend off tacklers, how to keep the ball and prevent it being spilt. The presentation of the ball is important, whether the ball carrier is still on his feet or has been dumped on the ground.

The player who is going to help must understand what options he has got. He can strip the ball carrier of the ball and go on himself; he can strip and pop the ball to a looping player; if the ball is insecure, he can go in and seal it off and wait for more help; if the ball has been spilt or placed, he can lift the ball and go; he can lift and pop up the ball to someone running faster than he is.

The ball should keep travelling in the same direction if it is recycled quickly. This takes it away from a fast-growing congested area into space. It takes it away from the forwards who are arriving from the previous phase of play. They will be put onside if the ball moves 5 metres from any mini-ruck or maul. If the three-quarters switch back, they will be running through stragglers who can now tackle them.

Lesson 13

Aim: to improve the ball-retention ability of the three-quarters.

Exercise 1

Fending off players. Work in pairs.

A player leans against his partner using one arm only. He has a ball in the other arm. He then pushes off and changes arm.

Progression: jogging down the pitch, side by side and passing a ball to each other. On the whistle, the player without the ball tries to tackle the ball carrier low. The ball carrier must fend him off.

Key points

● Hand on tackler's head, shoulder or chest.

● Straighten arm.

● Push away.

● Lean on the tackler and push your own hips and legs away from his outstretched arms.

[7-10 minutes]

Exercise 2

Preventing the ball from being spilt in the tackle.

In pairs 2 metres apart with a ball between them.

Player 1 is in the front support position (a 'line-backer'). On the signal, he is to pick up the ball and drive into his partner who is standing close to the ball. The ball must not be spilt.

Progression (i): in fives. One player faces four who are in an arc formation. The lone player has a ball and is holding a tackle shield. The coach shouts a number and the nominated player hits the shield. The ball must not be spilt.

Progression (ii): a gauntlet of players. A line of ball carriers is to run through the corridor as the players try to slap the ball out of their hands.

Progression (iii): in threes. Player 1 tries to catch player 2. Player 3 stays between them carrying a ball. Player 3 fends off 1 and protects 2.

The full-back is tackled and fights to stay on his feet for as long as possible. The ball is under control so that if he goes to ground he will be able to make it available to his support

Key points

- Dip shoulder and lead with one shoulder ahead of the other.
- Hold ball firmly on outside of chest.
- Contact with hand and forearm and push away.

[10 minutes]

Exercise 3

In fives with a ball. Go in successive waves; a cyclic exercise.

The ball is passed along the line. On the signal from the coach, the ball carrier stops as if tackled and presents the ball to the player who passed it to him. The passer must go in, take the ball and immediately make a pass outside, perhaps to another player inside him who is now looping to the outside.

For example, 1 has passed to 2 and 2 to 3. Coach shouts 'Tackle' and 3 stops and presents the ball. Player 2 goes in and strips him of it and pops the ball up to 1, who has come around on the loop to inject some pace into the movement again. He now makes a pass to 4, 4 to 5 and 5 back inside to 4, etc., and the cycle continues over a longish distance.

Start at a jogging pace, then shorten the distance and speed up the action.

Progression (i): on the tackle the ball carrier puts the ball down on the ground. The passer of the ball goes in and lifts the ball. Either he runs on or he pops it up to a looping player.

Progression (ii): on the tackle the ball carrier puts the ball down. The passer of the ball acts as a scrum-half and everyone re-positions himself and re-aligns during a count to five. The new scrum-half distributes the ball.

Key points

- Ball carrier runs straight and keeps his hips square.
- He must turn inside towards his support so that they can see the ball all the time, and at no stage should the ball be hidden by his back.
- The passer of the ball should take the responsibility of seeing the ball through the tackled player's hands. He must go in and help, and understand what options he has got.
- Three-quarters support three-quarters

● ·Keep going in the same direction. Attack the far side of the ruck or maul.

● Each three-quarter should get use to playing out of position and receiving a pass from the scrum-half.

● Each three-quarter should try to slot in wherever he can, but there must be communication so that wherever he is coming into the line, the player inside steps in and the player outside steps out to give him room (*see* the lesson on looping).

[10-12 minutes]

Exercise 4

Either three-quarter line against three-quarter line or 4 v 4. Full contact, and to be played in a restricted space.
    The ball to be returned to the coach each time so that he can re-start the game any way he likes.

Key points

● Keep position.

● Stay on your feet.

● Three-quarters support three-quarters. Go and help the tackled player.

[15 minutes]

MIDFIELD AND BACK-ROW LINK: LESSON 14

From set-piece possession and by means of a number of tactics, the midfield try to commit the opposition to the tackle near or beyond the gain line. The intention is to disrupt their defensive organisation. Ways of doing this are switches, bringing in the blind-side winger, a short pass from fly-half to inside centre who has changed his angle of run, the fly-half taking a flat pass from the scrum-half.

Communication with the back row is important so that they know where to head for and who is involved in the initial strike.

If the field is divided into four channels, the back row can be told which channel the three-quarters are going for. By calling

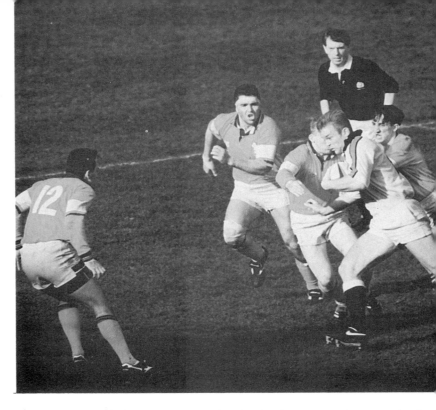

'the number of the player involved, the back row know which player they have to watch and aim for. This should give them an advantage over the opposition back row and they should have less trouble in getting to the breakdown more quickly than their opponents.

The open-side flanker should be there first. Depending on what has happened at the tackle, he has several options. He may have to secure the ball; he may have to rip the ball out and pop it up to the no. 8 to continue the movement; the ball may have been spilt and require lifting off the ground; the ball may be next to the tackled player and he may have to step over and be the front player of a ruck.

The general rule is that the three-quarter involved will try to stay on his feet and turn inside towards (not away from) his support. No.7 should strip him of the ball so that he can get out to re-join his line.

The back row should try to take the ball a little further on from the initial tackle area.

There are problems if the ball has been dropped in midfield or the three-quarters fail to get near the gain line. This means that the back row will have to run back to secure the ball. This too should be practised.

Get forwards running at three-quarters! The intention is to disrupt the organised defences and commit three-quarters to the tackle. Let the three-quarters have a quick ball after this, before the defenders can re-organise

Lesson 14

Aim: the midfield takes the tackle line close to the gain line from set-piece possession and links with the back row.

Exercise 1

In threes. The coach has a supply of balls. Channels are marked out with cones. Coach rolls ball into any one of the channels.

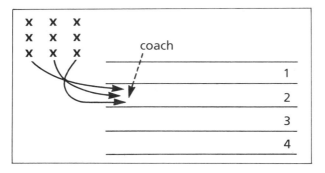

First player of the first group is to feed the next one who will run down that channel. All of them get in behind and play off each other with pop-up passes or rolling mauls or drives until they get to the end of that particular channel.

Key points

⬦ Take the ball down the same channel as the one where the tackle takes place or ball is retrieved. That is where the hole in the defence has been made.

⬦ Back row works together. There has to be communication between them.

[7-10 minutes]

Exercise 2

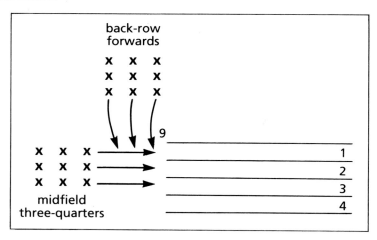

The three-quarters are arranged into threes opposite the channels. They are arranged in several waves. The back row is also arranged in threes and in waves.

The scrum-half passes a ball to the first set of three-quarters, who make switches and loops, etc. into a channel and then put the ball down or hold it up as if in a tackle on the signal from the coach. First back row strips the ball carrier and plays down the same channel.

Progression: put tackle shield holders in each of the channels so that contact with opposition in midfield is a little more realistic.

Key points

⬦ Midfield players try to stay on their feet in the tackle.

Midfield players turn inwards towards the back row. Do not present your back to them.

Back row players strip the three-quarter of the ball to release him to get back into position.

Back row players get beyond the tackler and put pace on the ball.

Back row players to be on the right side of the ball, so the midfield should have communicated to them first where they were striking and then who was doing it.

[15-20 minutes]

Exercise 3

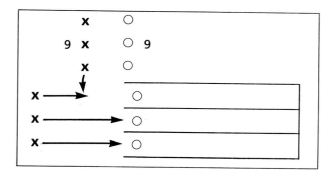

Put a back row and midfield in opposition. Holding tackles. Defending back row get behind the tackle so that attackers have to get through. Attack the same channel as the ball carrier was tackled in. Back row go 10 metres and each is to handle the ball. Now give to scrum-half to give back to the three-quarters.

Key points

Midfield to communicate with the back row.

The ball carrier should run straight and step inside towards his back row.

When tackled the ball carrier should turn inside towards his back row. He should not present his back to them.

Advance the tackle line as close to the gain line as possible. (This requires looking at another lesson plan on alignment, so for the purposes of this exercise get the defenders to be less competitive and allow the attackers to get near the gain line.)

● Back row strip the ball carrier of the ball and take it on further down the same channel and through the hole created.

[15-20 minutes]

Exercise 4

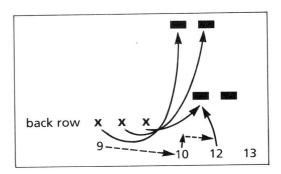

Midfield players bring the ball back and make contact with first line of shields. Open-side flanker takes the short cut and rips ball from the ball carrier. He then gives a 'gut' pass to the no. 8 who carries the ball forwards to the second line of shields. He makes contact and the other two members of the back row join him. They can both cross bind and leave the ball carrier to go to ground if he wants. He may wish to post the ball on the ground or create a maul and then distribute to the scrum-half. The three-quarters re-align to attack either left or right.

Progression (i): put the second line of shields closer to the first line so reaction time is reduced.

Progression (ii): put the second line on the open side of the first line. Open-side flanker to give a pop pass to the no. 8.

MIDFIELD AND BACK-ROW LINK: LESSON 15

Lesson 15

Aim: the midfield players are looking for support from their forwards.

Exercise 1

A back row with a midfield against a similar group, i.e. 6 v 6. Two channels are marked out, each about 10 metres apart. Three defenders in each channel, spread about that channel so there are plenty of gaps to attack. Three attackers at the head of each channel.

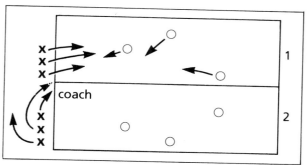

If the coach gives the ball to the attackers in channel 1, then only channel 1 is to be used; the same applies for channel 2. If the coach gives the ball to the attackers in channel 1, only the defenders in channel 1 can defend, those in channel 2 remaining where they are. However, the attackers in channel 2 come round into channel 1, coming from deep, reading the situation developing in front of them. The attack therefore becomes 6 v 3.

Before the breakdown occurs, the ball carrier should be looking for his support coming from deep. The support should be trying to read what is happening in front so that they can be effective in continuing the attack.

Key points

⬤ Initial attackers move the defenders around with passes and different angles of run.

⬤ Ball carrier should be looking for his support.

⬤ Support comes from deep and times his run to advance the ball further.

⬤ If the tackle takes place, the support should strip the ball carrier and take the ball on.

⬤ Communication should take place between the ball carrier and the support.

[15 minutes]

Exercise 2: midfield has failed to get across the gain line

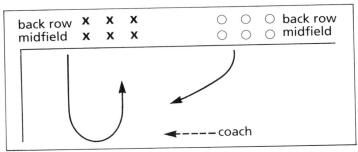

Six against six. The groups are about 15 metres apart and all lined up on the goal line facing downfield.

The coach rolls the ball into the area in front of them. The attackers run out to secure the ball and turn to attack the goal line. The midfield secures the ball first and the back row plays off them. The defenders try to prevent the score on the coach's signal by the back row going to the ball and the three-quarters defending against three-quarters.

Progression (i): the back row secures the ball, the three-quarters spread, and the ball is delivered to them when the opposition has been sucked in. The back row plays off the three-quarters again.

Progression (ii): defenders are called A or B. A = back row, B = three-quarters. Coach calls A or B and the nominated group comes out to defend. If A, then back row defends against back row. If B, then midfield defends against midfield, and attackers read situation. If no one is in front, go forwards and if opposed, give to the three-quarters.

Progression (iii): call out A and B but stagger them so that they arrive at different times.

Key points

- First secure the ball.
- Take the tackle and stay on your feet.
- Three-quarters look for a forward.
- Forwards strip a three-quarter of the ball.

[20 minutes]

Exercise 3: revision of midfield three-quarters being tackled near the gain line from set-piece possession.

Again, back row plus midfield three-quarters opposed by similar formation. Break up midfield defence and look to back row. Back row gets beyond midfield defence. Inside centre steps in and presents ball to back row. Starting positions as for a line-out or scrum. Each back-row player starts on his knees.

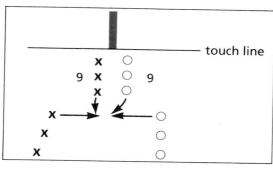

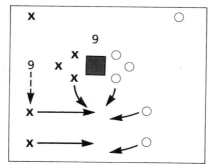

Key points

● Do not run across, presenting your back to the back row. Run straight.

● Stay on your feet in the tackle and look for a forward.

● Turn inwards in the tackle to present the ball to your back row.

● Keep communication between three-quarters and back row so that the back row knows which channel and which player they need to head towards.

● Take the ball from a three-quarter and take the ball forwards.

[20 minutes]

CHAPTER 6

Broken play and the narrow side

THE RUNNING/PASSING OPTION: LESSON 16

The laws introduced in 1992 regarding the ruck and maul have made it even more important to include a good decision maker at no. 10. Whoever takes the ball into contact situations has a responsibility to ensure that the ball re-emerges quickly. Defenders, knowing this, do not have to commit themselves to the breakdown and can stand off the rucks and mauls. There are more players to contend with at second phase and the fly-half's ability to count up numbers and see space is vital.

Players have to be helped to see. Heads should be up, scanning the field in front. They should be constantly asking questions of themselves: Where is the space? Where are the gaps? How much time do we have? Do we outnumber the defenders?

If outnumbered, the fly-half may decide to kick, but where he kicks and what type of kick he employs are also areas of concern. The team must have an overall kicking strategy.

Coaches differ over whether the fly-half, having taken the decision to run at the defenders, takes a flat pass or takes the ball deep from the scrum-half. These views are not irreconcilable. The further out the space or hole in the defence, the deeper the fly-half takes the ball. What matters is the passing line. Can the next player get his pass in? Give him enough time to do that and fix the defender by running at his inside shoulder; that is then the correct passing line.

Communication with the scrum-half is essential. This must be by verbal signals. The scrum-half tends to be looking to his front most of the time, ball watching. He cannot afford much time to look back to find out where the fly-half will be. Many half-back pairings will have played together a great deal and will have built up a good working relationship to the point that they generally understand what their partner wants. However, the rule of thumb is that as the fly-half starts his run he will shout out a signal indicating the side he is running to.

If the loose play is on the edges of the field, the fly-half will have little alternative as to where he first takes up his position. If there are options, however, it is wise not to signal where you are going too early. The fly-half might decide to stand behind the loose, and he can then keep the opposition guessing as to what his intentions are. He might decide to stand to the left and run to the right on an arc, or vice versa.

Lesson 16

Aim: to improve the decision making of the midfield three-quarters from second phase possession.

Exercise 1

In groups of five – three attackers and two defenders. Passive opposition to start with so that the attackers can get their lines of running correct and also the timing of the pass. Over an area of 10 x 10 metres.

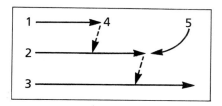

Player 1 has the ball and runs at 4 and times his pass to 2. Player 5 has come out and 2 times his pass to 3 having fixed 5. The defenders take man-for-man and do not drift out. Jog through to the far side of the grid, turn round and get ready to come back.

Progression (i): 5 stands in the second channel, thus giving 1 and 2 less time to get their passes away.

Progression (ii): 1 is told to run too far so that he puts 2 under pressure to get his pass away. Player 2 now has to decide whether he has time to pass or whether he should hold on to the ball, take the tackle and wait for help.

Progression (iii): 5 poses problems for the attackers. He can either drift on to the outside player or stay man-for-man. Player 2 has to decide whether to pass or dummy and go himself.

Mental rehearsal! Running through in your mind a brief checklist of key factors before taking the kick will pay dividends. Head down; hands underneath the ball; place the ball on the foot; kick through the target; left hand to right foot

*Head steady and down; left hand to right foot; left shoulder kept tight –
if it swings away it pulls the body and hips through the rotational axis
and the power of the kick does not go through the ball, rather the ball
swings away and length is lost*

Key points

- Aim at the defender's inside shoulder to fix him.

- Do not pass so late that the next player cannot get his pass away.

- If a player is caught in possession of the ball, the player who passed to him must go in and rip and go, or give a soft, short pass to the outside player.

- If you feel the pressure on you, make the pass; if you feel the pressure on the outside player, hold on to the ball and dummy.

- End player to hang back and accelerate on to pass.

[15 minutes]

Exercise 2

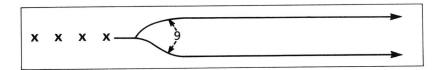

Scrum-half is fed a supply of balls by another scrum-half. A succession of players take the ball running and call out which side and how far out, e.g. 'wide right' or 'close left', etc.

Progression (i): two lines of players, each line numbered 1 or 2.

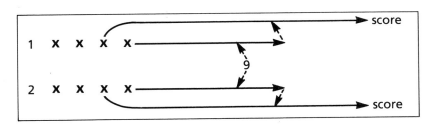

When coach calls '1 and 1', two from the first line are to come out and receive a pass from the scrum-half; the receiver is then to pass on to the second nominated player, who scores. The coach can call '1 and 2'; '2 and 2'; '2 and 1'. The first player nominated receives the first pass; the other has to get outside him to receive a pass from him.

The scrum-half pass from line-out ball. Head, eyes, hands and feet are all pointing towards the target. Keep a low body position in the follow-through

Progression (ii): now with two shield holders as tacklers.

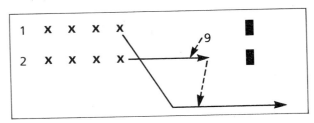

Opposition to knock ball down, bump or holding tackles. Support must re-position on ball carrier.

Key points

🏈 Verbal communication from fly-half to scrum-half.

🏈 First attacking player to run at the first defender and fix him so that he cannot drift out on to the second attacker.

🏈 How far away from the defender does the first ball carrier make his pass? Not so close that he is tackled with the ball. Not so far that the defender has time to move across into the second attacker's path.

[15 minutes]

Exercise 3

A progression from the previous exercise.

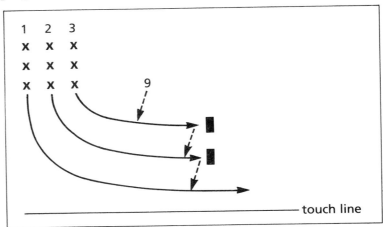

Coach calls '1,2,3' or '1,1,1' or '2,3,1', etc. Whatever the combination of numbers, the first nominated player receives the pass from the scrum-half, the second nominated receives a pass from the first nominated and the third receives the last pass.

Key points

- Communication with the scrum-half.

- Run on an arc to straighten the line and fix the defenders, or crab sideways quickly and then start running forwards and straight at inside shoulders.

- Get on the outside of the defender and attack his inside shoulder.

- Get outside shoulder pointing inwards towards the ball. This will straighten up hips and running lines.

- Visually pick up your defender first before looking for the ball.

- Fix the defender before making the pass. Do not pass too early or too late.

- If the ball is received deep, this would allow a second line of defence to get up and across.

- If the pass is made deep, this would allow the first line of defence to drift on to the outside players.

- The spacing between players should not be too wide. This allows miss passes to be effective.

- If the pressure is on the ball carrier, he should pass; if the pressure is on the outside player, the ball carrier should hold on and attack the gap.

[15 minutes]

MORE DECISION-MAKING: LESSON 17

Lesson 17

Aim: to improve the decision-making at fly-half from second phase possession.

Exercise 1

One scrum-half can be fed the ball by another so that they can always change over for a rest.

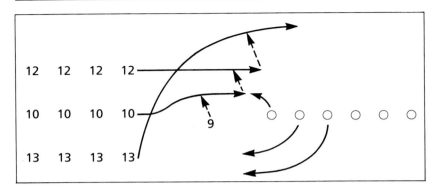

Waves of midfield players are confronted by a loose maul/ruck so that they can attack either side of it. There is a centre on either side of the fly-half so he can use either one. The decision as to which side to attack is made by the fly-half, who reacts to the defenders.

The defenders are lined up in threes.

The defenders are told that they are to step out into the channels on either side of the loose on the signal from the coach. However, all three are not to go to the same side at once. One must go one side and two must go the other. The fly-half goes to the less well defended side, i.e. where there is only one defender. Here he fixes the defender and makes a pass to his centre. If he takes the wrong decision, the centre on the far side must try to get outside him so that it will be a 3 v 2 situation rather than 2 v 2.

Progression: put a winger with each centre and have four defenders. Two go one way and two go the other so that it is always 3 v 2. The fly-half has to time his release of the ball.

Key points

● Scan the field and go to the less well defended side.

● Run on an arc to straighten, and run at the defender to fix him.

● The depth at which the fly-half takes the ball depends on his estimation of the passing line. If the space is on the wing, can the inside players fix the defenders and get away their passes?

[20 minutes]

Exercise 2

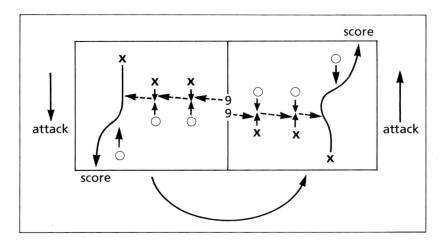

When the attackers have beaten the defence in front of them, they move into the next channel. Change positions with the defenders at regular intervals. The first two attackers fix the first two defenders and the third attacker beats the third defender by footwork or a chip kick.

Progression (i): the third attacker takes the last defender wide and plays back inside to support.

Progression (ii): third attacker comes back inside to bring last defender infield. He then makes an outward switch with a support runner.

Progression (iii): first attacker fixes first defender and gives a long pass to third attacker. How do they score now?

Progression (iv): first two attackers dummy switch and give a pass to third attacker. Play to score.

Progression (v): second defender is allowed to vary his defence. Decisions have to be made by second attacker.

Progression (vi): both defenders to vary their defence. The third defender takes the fly-half if he breaks. Play to score.

Progression (vii): third defender closes down the space very quickly. Second attacker may have to chip/grub kick the ball into the space behind him.

Slow ball! The fly-half at the end of this pass has only one option – to kick. He is receiving the ball deep, directly behind the loose play and the defenders have had time to fan out and organise themselves

Key points

● If the space is wide out, the fly-half will pass early so that the centres can get in their passes – but not so early and so deep that the defenders can just drift across and fill in the hole.

● If the gap is closed in, the fly-half will take the ball flatter and hold on to the ball a little longer.

● What matters is the passing line in relation to the tackle line 1.

[20 minutes]

Exercise 3

Two sets of three-quarters. The coach, with a ball, wanders across the pitch and sometimes forwards and backwards. The scrum-half of each team stays with him. Everyone has to re-position themselves on the ball.

The coach will call in two defenders to him. When they are there or as they are approaching, he releases the ball to the attacking scrum-half who immediately passes to the fly-half.

The fly-half has to spot the gaps and space, and his team tries to score.

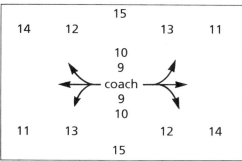

Progression: if the attacking unit does not score and there is a breakdown, the coach shouts 'Tackle' and all the attackers have to head for the coach who has now secured the ball at the breakdown. As the attackers home in towards him, the coach gives the ball to the other unit who now counter-attack. Previous attackers now become defenders once the ball has gone to the scrum-half.

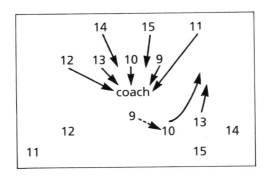

Key points

- Count the numbers.
- See the space.
- Note well the passing line in relation to the tackle line.
- Fix defenders by running at them at pace.

[20 minutes]

CHAPTER 7

Going over the defence

THE BOMB: LESSON 18

The high kick into the box in front of the forwards tends to be executed by the fly-half. While he usually makes this kick towards the posts, the inside centre will often use it as well.

Much depends on the quality of possession and the time and space available. The advantage of the inside centre taking the high kick to the posts from a line-out is that he will be under less pressure than the fly-half, and he will be just on the inside of the channel where he intends placing the kick. This will help with the accuracy of the kick.

From both sides of the pitch, if the player taking the kick is the one just on the inside of the targeted channel, he can face downfield all the time. His hips will be square, the follow-through will tend not to be across the body and he will get greater height and length from the kick.

The advantage of this type of kick is that there is a good chance of recovering possession. Designated chasers and sweepers are important, however. If the fly-half kicks to the box, the winger and the inside centre must chase. If the fly-half kicks to the posts then the two centres must chase. The first one to the ball contests possession and the other sweeps for loose or spilt ball.

If the ball is not cleanly recovered by catching it or tapping it down to the sweeper, the defending player who catches the ball should be smothered. The ball should be tackled.

For the kick back to the box for the winger to chase, the winger must understand that if the catcher has time to take the ball and find touch, then he must try to cut down the angle of the kick and attack the kicking leg. His approach would usually be infield, pushing the kicker to the touch lines.

The centre who is chasing should be aware that he is also being used to cut out a counter-attack. If the defending winger catches the ball, he may decide on a long pass to his own full-back for him either to kick to touch or to launch a counter-attack. The centre has to counter both options.

The kick to the posts is a difficult kick to clear for the defence. It is a long way to either touch line.

The scrum-half kicks into the box on either side of the field for his winger to run on to. The advantage of him taking this kick is that he is already ahead of the fly-half and it is therefore possible to advance further into opposition territory. The opposition has less reaction time and has to run deeper by some 10 metres than for a kick from the fly-half.

To make the kicking strategy simple, on the left-hand side of the field let the fly-half kick; on the right side let the scrum-half kick.

Lesson 18

Aim: to use the high kick as a tactical weapon and get players to chase it.

Exercise 1

A ball between two players, kicking high to each other.

Progression: time how long the ball is in the air. Measure the greatest distance a player can run while the ball is in the air its optimum time. He would arrive at the ball's landing spot at the same time.

A rough guide is that the ball should be in the air one second plus one for every 10 metres. For example, if the ball is to travel 20 metres, for a chasing player to arrive at the same time as the ball, the hang time for the ball will be 2 + 1 = 3 seconds; for 30 metres it will be 3 + 1 = 4 seconds, etc.

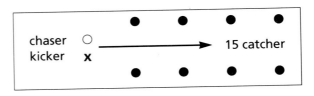

In twos, one to kick the bomb, the other to chase. A full-back to receive the ball can be placed on the 10, 20, 30 or 40 metre lines which have been marked out by cones.

Time the hang time with a stopwatch and work out optimum distances for each player so they know their capabilities.

Dealing with the bomb: eyes focused on the ball; elbows tucked in; one shoulder leading and beyond the ball; one foot in front to provide stability

Key points

- Hips at slight angle before the kick.

- Hips end up square in the kick. There should be little rotation at hips in the kick.

- Shoulders square. Close the left shoulder. Left shoulder should not drop; keep it tight so that it does not swing loose (if kicking with right foot).

- Long back-swing with leg. A 90° angle at the knee of the kicking foot (back of calf and back of knee).

- Wide angle between both legs.

- Left hand to right foot but the arm should not come across the body.

- Both hands under ball at each end of ball. This gives a free spot on the ball for foot to kick through.

- Place the ball on the foot.

- Point ball away and downwards.

- Drive hips forwards before unleashing the kick.

- Hit belly of ball with top of foot.

- Point toes downwards.

- Keep head down after ball has gone.

[15 minutes]

Exercise 2

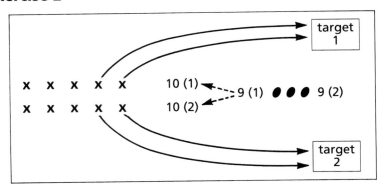

Two scrum-halves with a supply of balls. One scrum-half is to feed the balls to the other. Two fly-halves, one on either side of the scrum-half. A line of players behind each fly-half. Two target areas – one for a box kick, one for a posts kick.

Scrum-half to pass to each fly-half in turn. The fly-half is to kick to his designated target area. The players lined up behind him are to go in pairs; one is to chase and the other is to sweep. If the ball is cleanly caught, a pass is to be made. If the ball is tapped back and collected, a pass has to be made after that. Return the ball. Occasionally rotate everyone.

Progression (i): put a defender in each target to deal with the kick.

Progression (ii): move the targets wider and add an inside centre to each fly-half. Get the fly-half to pass to him and he is to kick.

Key points

● Kicking as for exercise 1.

● The chaser goes slightly beyond the ball to gather it or tap back. Lead with one shoulder and arm to prevent a knock-on.

● The chaser should try to get the first touch, so get off the ground if possible.

● If the defender secures the ball first, tackle the ball and wait for help from the sweeper.

● The sweeper has to read the situation and decide whether he can run on to a pass. Gather the loose ball; go and secure the ball from the chaser who is finding it difficult to play it.

[15-20 minutes]

Exercise 3

A game with seven balls in total and seven players in each side. Each team in a grid with a grid between them. They are to kick bombs to each other non-stop. The coach counts how many are dropped or miss their targets and keeps a running score. First to ten wins.

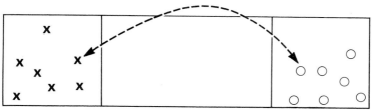

Key points

● Kicks as for exercise 1.

● Receivers keep their eyes on the ball and call for it. The player at the back has priority.

● Reach for the ball. Keep elbows in.

● One foot in front of the other and stand side-on to withstand a tackle (there are none in this exercise) and also so that if the ball is dropped it will go backwards.

[15 minutes]

BOX KICK BY SCRUM-HALF: LESSON 19

Lesson 19

Aim: to improve the scrum-half's kicking into the box.

Exercise 1

Scrum-halves in pairs with 5–10 balls between them. One scrum-half kicks while the other retrieves the balls.

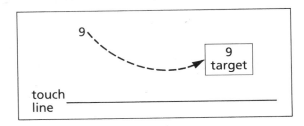

Set up a small grid as a target area. Scrum-half kicks into this. The receiving partner catches every ball no matter where and places each ball on the ground where it has landed. Look at the grouping. Try to achieve consistency.

Progression (i): put the target on the other side as if the scrum-half is at the base of a scrum on the left side of the field. He would then have to kick over the forwards.

Progression (ii): competition between the scrum-halves, who take it in turns to see how many balls they can land inside a small target area. Best of 20 kicks.

Key points

⬤ First get in position as if to pass.

⬤ Take one long step back to make room.

⬤ Lean back and kick around the corner off the top of the foot.

⬤ You will be facing the touch line on the right-hand side of the field. On the left side you will be more at an angle and turned towards the opposition's posts.

⬤ Kick the centre of the ball.

⬤ Stroke the ball, do not jab at it. Follow through as if it is a golf swing.

[20-30 minutes]

Exercise 2

In a largish group of 9–13 with a supply of balls. A scrum-half to do the kicking, but now under some pressure. Use a target area with a retriever in it. One player acts as a no. 8. He places a ball at his feet each time for the scrum-half to pick up and kick. Another player acts as a blind-side flanker and tries to make the kick difficult as soon as the scrum-half picks up.

A supply of right wingers go in turn and chase the kicks to arrive at the same time as the ball, or pressurise the receiver. There is a supply of receivers who take it in turns in the grid. Receiver and winger rotate positions. Also rotate 8 and 6, and change the scrum-halves.

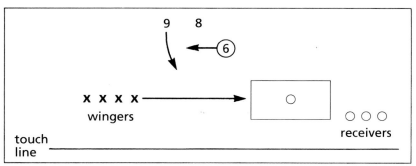

Progression: two chasers, one acting as a winger and the other as a centre. Two receivers, one acting as a winger and the other as a full-back. If the defenders have time to counter-attack, they are to do so while the chasers try to prevent it. Either proper tackling or touch tackles.

Key points

- The kick as for exercise 1.

- The chasers as for exercise 2.

- Chasers approach on outside of receiver and drive him towards touch-line if he retrieves the ball with time to spare. Attack his stronger leg.

- The receivers as for exercise 2.

- *See* lessons on counter-attack.

[15-25 minutes]

THE WIPERS KICK: LESSON 20

This is the long diagonal kick from a line-out or a scrum on either side of the field. Sometimes its purpose is to roll the ball into touch to make ground, although possession is thereby lost. More usually it is intended to put the ball in the corners or near the touch line and put the defenders under pressure. They will then have to find touch. Their angle will not be wide; possibly they may be outside their own 22-metre zone and unable to kick directly to touch. The resulting kick will mean that the attacking side has probably gained ground and they have retained possession because they get the throw-in.

Who is the best player to take this kick to the far touch line or corner? The fly-half has taken this kick by tradition. The inside centre came to be regarded as the best player because the defending open-side winger could hang back to cover a kick from the fly-half but could not afford to wait for the inside centre to pass before coming up on his own winger. Consequently it was felt that if the inside centre took the kick, he could place it behind the defending winger. However, the outside centre is now being used more often to take this kick. He is just inside this channel and can kick more parallel to touch and deeper inside the opposition's territory. The defending winger has come up even further, leaving even more space behind him. It is now no longer quite such a diagonal kick but the aim is to put the ball in a similar area and for similar reasons as the old wipers kick.

Who takes the kick will depend on who can kick with accuracy and whether there are left-footers in the side. If, for example, there is a line-out on the right side of the field and there is a left-footed kicker in the three-quarters, move him to outside centre. If the ball is moved wide to him, he can kick along the left touch line towards the left corner.

Designated chasers are necessary to put the defence under pressure. The first one to the ball contests for re-possession, while the other acts as a sweeper to recover spilt ball. The open-side winger is the best placed player to chase. Perhaps the other chaser could be the inside centre or even the full-back (with the inside centre or blind-side winger dropping back to cover the full-back's position). So much depends on the players in the team, their preferences and abilities, that the pattern of kicker and chasers will vary from team to team.

The defender who has to deal with the kick will generally find the ball rolling behind him. If under pressure, he will have to kick to touch with the leg further from the chaser, i.e. with the left foot to the left touch and the right foot to the right touch line. His angle is much reduced as a result. If under less pressure or if able to side-step the chaser, he can widen the angle to kick off his right leg to the left touch and left to the right touch line.

Lesson 20

Aim: to improve the tactical kicking to the corners and the defending against such kicks.

Exercise 1

In pairs with a ball. Players stand 10 metres apart. Simple punting to each other, striving for accuracy and developing technique.

Progression: to get them moving to the catch and to speed up the kicking and get more of a diagonal kick, put them at either end of a grid.

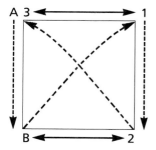

Player B kicks across the diagonal to position 1 and runs to position 2. Player A runs to position 1, catches and kicks the ball to position 2 for B to catch. B kicks across the diagonal for A to catch at position 3. He catches and kicks to B who has returned to his starting position. So B kicks down the side of the grid while A kicks the diagonal.

Key points

🏈 The body should face the direction of the kick.

🏈 Keep the head down even after the kick.

🏈 Keep shoulders and hips square; there should no rotation of these in the kick.

🏈 Hold the ball with the right hand at the nearer end and under the ball. The left hand is at the far end of the ball and also under it.

🏈 Hold the ball waist high and release it on to the top of the foot.

🏈 Point the toes downwards.

🏈 Follow through. Do not stab at the ball.

[15 minutes]

Exercise 2

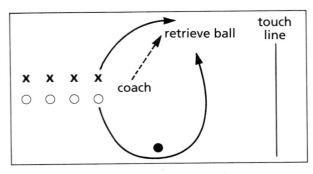

Coach, with a supply of balls, rolls them into the 22-metre zone and in the right-hand corner (for the attackers). Each defender in turn picks up and finds touch by stepping back inside and kicking off the right foot and then later by turning slightly and kicking off his left foot to the left touch line. The kick can be first a punt and later a grubber kick.

Progression: add chasers. When the coach rolls the ball, the retriever's partner sets off around a marker and puts pressure on the defending kick.

Key points

⬤ If the ball is rolling away, chase and wait for it to pop up if you have time.

⬤ It may be necessary to fall on the ball and bounce up.

⬤ If you are under pressure it may be better to keep your back to the opposition; this will also prevent a knock-on. The best approach is from the side where it is possible to have some field of vision, and yet the danger of a knock-on is less than if facing fully to the front.

⬤ If the ball is rolling towards you, bend your knees and get your whole body in the way. Let it roll up into your forearms and the crook of your elbows. You may also consider trapping it with your foot before picking up.

⬤ If you are under pressure, kick with the leg that is further from the chaser and closer to the touch line.

⬤ If there is time, feint to kick and step back inside to give yourself more time and a better angle to kick off the leg further from touch.

⬤ The chaser should approach in a hockey-stick fashion, driving the retriever towards touch, cutting down his angle and also attacking the kicking leg.

[15 minutes]

Exercise 3

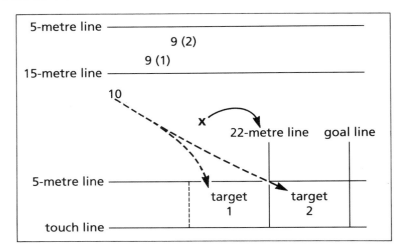

In fives to tens with a target about 30 metres away on a diagonal from the kickers. The fly-half receives a pass from the scrum-half. He kicks the diagonal to the target. Decide whether he has to find touch with the rolling ball or get it as close to the touch line as possible and just outside the 22-metre line. This is target 1. Target 2 is as close to the touch line and as close to the goal line as possible.

Chasers allow the ball to come to rest. One then brings the ball back to the scrum-half position to act as a scrum-half. The fly-half now goes to the queue of chasers, and the scrum-half takes his place. The second scrum-half passes to him and they all rotate again.

Progression: place a queue of defenders at X. They are to take it in turns to retrieve the rolling ball behind them and find touch despite the attentions of the chaser.

Key points

🏉 Kickers as for exercise 1.

🏉 Chasers approach from the inside to drive the defender towards the touch line and narrow his angle. Attack his kicking leg.

🏉 Receivers as for exercise 2.

[15 minutes]

CHAPTER 8

Counter-attack

The full-back has his eyes focused on the ball and cannot safely scan the field in front of him. One of the wingers has to get behind him and serve as his eyes. He is the decision maker. He tells the full-back whether he has time to find touch, or catch and run, or pass it to him on his left or right.

The second winger drops slightly further back directly behind the full-back. He is to sweep up any spilt ball or tapped-on possession.

The chasers of the ball are homing in on the full-back and if he can catch the ball and distribute it to the winger who is taking it on the run and to the side, these chasers should be outflanked. The winger must be careful not to overrun the full-back lest he hurries him into making a bad or forward pass.

The ball must be brought forwards as quickly as possible to close the distance between it and the rest of the team.

While the ball was in the air, the midfield players should have been turning and dropping back. They can create an umbrella of safety for the full-back by closing towards him and making it difficult for the chasers of the kick to get through to tackle him. Do not blatantly obstruct!

Run towards opposition strength and work the ball towards the space.

Lesson 21

Aim: to improve the counter-attacking capability of the back three.

Exercise 1

A ball between two players, one on the touch line and his partner on the 5-metre line. The player on the touch line has the ball and throws it high in the air to his partner, who is to

The ball is retrieved. A counter-attack is to be launched by a single pass to a support player who communicated that decision to the passer while he was concentrating on the ball

catch it. In the meantime the thrower runs behind the receiver and on to his pass, bringing the ball back towards the touch line again.

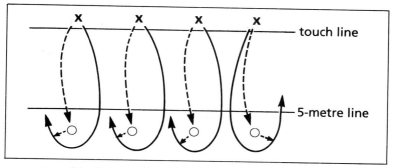

Progression (i): the catcher can join in the counter-attack and receive a pass on the way back towards the starting position.

Progression (ii): both start on the touch line. One rolls the ball towards the 5-metre line for his partner to run after, pick up and pass the ball quickly to him as he again times the run.

Key points

🌰 Support player is to communicate with the catcher. Tell him exactly where he is and how you want the ball and when.

🌰 Time the run so that you are not standing still when it is passed.

🌰 Time the run when the ball is in the catcher's hands and he is ready to pass.

[10 minutes]

Exercise 2

Use a grid 20 metres long by 15 metres wide. 4 v 4 (i.e. two at the back and two at the front).

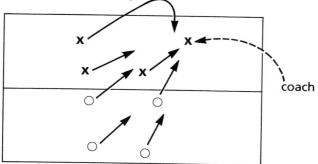

The coach kicks or throws the ball to either side but always to the two players who are deep. One fields the ball and the other starts the counter-attack. One-handed touch tackles to start with. Once a player is touched, a pass has to be made immediately.

Key points

⬤ The fielder of the ball is not the decision maker.

⬤ The support player gets in behind the fielder and takes decisions.

⬤ Bring the ball forwards quickly.

⬤ Time the run when the fielder can offer the pass.

⬤ Communicate with the fielder.

⬤ The players in midfield get back, providing initial umbrella cover, and then get into support positions.

[15 minutes]

Exercise 3

A game of rugby baseball.

The players of the kicking side take it in turns to kick a ball from under the posts into the field of play. The kick must stay in play. After taking the kick, the player must run and pick up another ball at a marker, run round two other markers and score a try anywhere on the goal line.

One team has to field. Their objective is to retrieve the ball which has been kicked. Each player in this team is to receive a pass and score on the goal line before the kicking side. If they do this before the kicker, the kicker is out. There are to be no forward passes or knock-ons. If the kicker scores first he scores one run.

Everyone has one kick each. Have two or more innings depending on the time available.

The distance the kicker has to run will vary with each age group and ability. If the kicker can kick long, the distance he has to run will also have to be long to give the retrievers some chance of getting him out.

A starting point would be to have the first marker on the 15-metre line where it meets the 22-metre line. Keep a supply of balls here and make it the point where the kicker has to pick up one. The second marker could be on the 10-metre line in the middle, and the third on the far 15-metre line where that meets the 22-metre line. This is the course to run before the kicker can score.

Key points

🏉 Bring the ball forwards as quickly as possible.

🏉 If you are in front of the ball, get back as quickly as you can. Work hard off the ball to get in a support position.

[20 minutes]

COUNTER-ATTACK PATTERN: LESSON 22

Lesson 22

Aim: to organise a counter-attacking pattern using the back three.

Exercise 1

In fours with a ball. Start on the 22- metre line. On the command, three of the four run forwards. The first player, with the ball, stays on the 22-metre line; the second runs to the near 10-metre line, the third to the half-way line and the fourth to the far 10-metre line.

The first player chip kicks the ball to the second player then runs forwards. The receiver of the kick gives a long pass to the third player and the third gives a long pass to the fourth player. The fourth player becomes scrum-half and passes the ball to the three who are running in support. They score on the far 22-metre line.

Key points

🏉 Move the ball to space with long passes.

🏉 Support after the pass.

[10 minutes]

Exercise 2

Work in threes in successive waves over a channel of 22 metres in width. Coach or kicker with a supply of balls to kick to each wave in turn. A counter-attack must be launched and a pattern worked out.

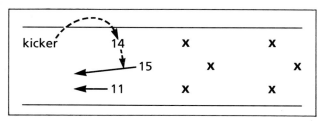

If the ball goes to the inside winger, he makes a long pass to the full-back who runs towards the kicker and makes a switch to the open side with the inside winger. That should leave both wingers attacking the space.

If the ball goes to the full-back, he switches with the inside winger after running back towards the kicker.

If the ball goes to the open-side winger, he runs towards the kicker and makes a dummy switch with the full-back and an orthodox switch with the inside winger.

Work out other patterns, but remember where the kick came from because that is where the forwards are.

Key points

● Counter-attack only if the kick is poor and the ball is immediately available.

● Dummy to strength by running towards congested areas.

● Take the ball to the space.

● Bring the ball forwards quickly.

[10 minutes]

Exercise 3

Five against three in a channel 22 metres wide.

Three players kick the ball out of defence to the five, who are counter-attacking by working the ball into space and the overlap rather than by individual evasion.

Key points

● Dummy to strength.

● Take the ball to the space.

● Receiver not to be the decision maker.

● Support player in behind the receiver takes the decisions.

● Bring the ball forwards quickly.

[15-20 minutes]

Exercise 3

A ball is kicked out of defence to a three-quarter unit which must counter-attack. This line will be opposed either by another three-quarter line acting as a set of forwards and appropriately lined up, or by a set of three-quarters in their normal starting and chasing positions.

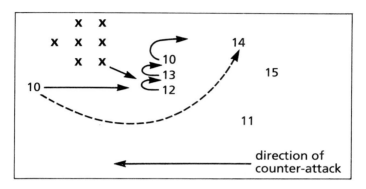

Key points

● Get back behind the ball as quickly as you can.

● Do not play around with the ball in midfield but get it across midfield quickly.

● Dummy to strength.

● Get the ball to the space.

● Bring the ball forwards quickly.

● The receiver of the ball should have immediate support behind him if it is a high kick.

[15-20 minutes]

FROM PINCHED BALL: LESSON 23

If the ball has been spilt in the tackle, there is an opportunity quickly to turn defence into attack.

The player picking up the ball will usually have lost momentum. There will be players lying around and in front of him. He may even be going backwards and unable to scan ahead and take decisions. He needs immediate support so that he can pass to someone who is running fast and is better placed to take decisions. That support must take the ball forwards quickly by coming from deep. If the tackle was made in midfield, the best player to pass to will be the blind-side winger or the full-back.

If the ball has been pinched in a maul, the three-quarters must work quickly to get back to their starting positions for an attack. If the ball is delivered to them quickly, the midfield have little time to get into a position where they can come forwards quickly again. They must get the ball wide as soon as possible to the open-side winger, who has more time to get deeper and run faster and more space in which to operate.

Try hard to change from a mentally defensive mode into an attacking one.

Lesson 23

Aim: to launch counter-attacks quickly from ball that has been pinched from the opposition.

Exercise 1

Five players jog very slowly towards their own goal line in a channel 20 metres wide. The first player passes the ball and runs in front of the other four players as they pass the ball back and forth. He decides when to come into the line and receive a pass. The rest of the line then turn and support him.

Progression: add three defenders who jog slowly behind the counter-attacking players. They should vary their formation.

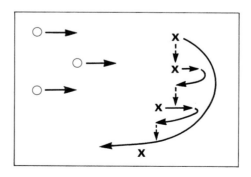

Key points

- Take the ball forwards quickly.
- Come from depth.

- Take the ball to space.

- The ball carrier is not the decision maker; this is the support player because he is facing the opposition.

- The ball carrier should not collide with the receiver.

- The counter-attacker is to communicate to the ball carrier where and when he wants the ball.

[10 minutes]

Exercise 2

Five versus five. Two channels, side by side and each about 10–15 metres wide. All the players are in one channel. The attackers have to score at the far end of that channel. The defence stops them either by orthodox tackles or by touch (with an immediate pass). The defenders can be instructed not to go for the ball.

When the attack has broken down, the coach throws another ball into the other channel and shouts 'Break'. The attackers run back and around a marker at their end of the channel and the defenders do the same at their end. The first to the ball launches a counter-attack. To help the team which is counter-attacking, the coach could roll the ball closer to their end of the channel.

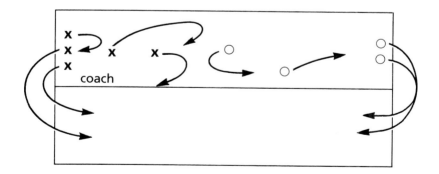

Key points

- First player to the ball should offer the ball to support.

- Support player should time the run so he can take the ball forwards quickly.

● Support player to communicate his decision to the retriever of the ball.

● Look for space and attack the gaps

[15-20 minutes]

Exercise 3

Two three-quarter lines, with one acting as a group of forwards. The three-quarter line forms a queue, and the forwards execute some close inter-passing and ball retention against them. When the defending three-quarter has been bumped and left behind, he should re-join the line at the end to continue offering token opposition.

When the coach shouts 'My ball', the forward who has the ball presents it to him and the three-quarters quickly get into attacking positions as he gives it to them and they counter-attack. The forwards oppose.

Progression: the three-quarters already in their normal positions. They back-pedal as the forwards jog towards them, inter-passing the ball. On the command 'Now', the forwards give the ball to the coach who gives it to the scrum-half. He sets his three-quarter line in motion as the forwards fan out and try to stop them scoring.

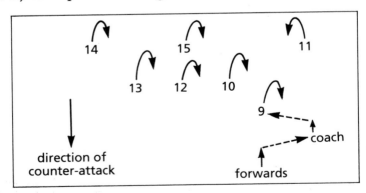

Key points

● Move the ball wide quickly with miss passes away from the pressure area.

● The players lying deep should attempt to get involved to get pace on the ball.

[15-20 minutes]

INDEX